Knowing and Doing God's Will

KNOWING AND DOING GOD'S WILL

JERRY GLISSON

BROADMAN PRESS
Nashville, Tennessee

© Copyright 1986 • Broadman Press
All Rights Reserved
4250-27
ISBN: 0-8054-5027-0
Dewey Decimal Classification: 231.5
Subject Heading: GOD—WILL
Library of Congress Catalog Number: 86-2617
Printed in the United States of America

Unless otherwise stated, all Scripture quotations are from the King James Version of the Bible.

Scripture quotations marked ASV are from the American Standard Version of the Bible.

Scripture quotations marked Phillips are reprinted with permission of Macmillan Publishing Co., Inc. from J. B. Phillips: *The New Testament in Modern English,* Revised Edition. © J. B. Phillips 1958, 1960, 1972.

Scripture quotations marked Berkeley are from *The Modern Language Bible, The New Berkeley Version.* Copyright 1945, 1959, © 1969 by Zondervan Publishing House. Used by permission.

Library of Congress Cataloging-in-Publication Data

Glisson, Jerry.
  Knowing and doing God's will.

  Bibliography: p.
  1. Christian life—Baptist authors.   2. God—Will.
I. Title.
BV4501.2.G575   1986   231.7   86-2617
ISBN 0-8054-5027-0

To my wife, Helen,
who seeks the will of God
along with me.
To the many who desire
some practical and simple guidelines
in seeking the will of God.

Contents

Preface

Foreword

Introduction.. 13

1. Receiving Divine Impressions..................... 23
2. Claiming the Promises 35
3. "Putting Out the Fleece" 47
4. Living Like the Lord Jesus 59
5. Doing the Will of God................................ 71
6. Receiving God's Truth 79
7. Knowing Who's Speaking 87
8. Operating Under the
   Holy Spirit's Leadership 103
9. Supernaturally Guided.............................. 115
10. Understanding the Will of Purpose 127
11. Discerning the Will of Desire 143
12. Grasping the Will of Permission 159

Epilogue.. 167

Notes.. 169

Preface

In 1951 Jerry Glisson wrote a doctoral dissertation entitled "The Will of God as Reflected in Greek Words." He could have used his research then and produced a book on the discovery of God's will. This could have been done long ago. I thank God that Dr. Glisson has waited until now to write his book.

He does not attempt to repeat the things that others have said. He believes that God is concerned in every area of the believer's life. He believes that God will reveal His will in all matters to believers who claim His will. This book comes from the pen of a Spirit-filled man who writes from experience. His experience in the will of God has been tried and demonstrated for many years. He has found in the Word of God directions to define and determine the will of God. He states, "The Bible has been given to enable us to learn God's sovereign will as well as His moral will." For many years Dr. Glisson has discovered God's will and this has made the power of God flow through his life.

Now he teaches us ways to know and experience the will of God. He states that he is attempting in this work to provide ways and means for a committed Christian to discover God's will in any area of concern. I pray that many will journey with him to the disclosure of God's will through the unhindered presence of the Holy Spirit.

Robert L. Hamblin

Foreword

The statement, "To know God's will is the greatest knowledge; to do God's will is the greatest achievement," is attributed to George W. Truett. No more concise or captivating truth was ever spoken. This book by my long-time friend, Jerry Glisson, will prove to be a great aid to the seeker of this great knowledge.

I have recently come upon ideas about the will of God that are somewhat bothersome. They fly in the face of what I have long been taught—that everything I do is within the realm of God's intense interest and desires. I do not enjoy thinking of God laughing at my prayers to know the exactness of His desires and will for my life because it really makes no difference to Him what I do. That has a ring of humanism that leaves me feeling empty.

With the skill of a theologian, the care of a father, and the precision of an engineer, Jerry Glisson walks us through the mine field of dangers safely and soundly to the will of God. His is no shallow "pop-theology" but biblical-based truth that has been tried in the crucible of experience in a seasoned pastor's life. He makes much of getting prepared to hear from God by coming to a purity of life before Him, an indespensably valid concept.

A high point in the book (one of many) is the chapter on "Living Like the Lord Jesus." Here the finish work comes into focus on the case for hearing from God in our daily lives.

His treatment of the *rhema* and *logos* is incomparable! It is a must for the seeking Christian. Just these words will begin the bells of freedom ringing:

> Logos is the Word; rhema is a word from the Word; logos is the message; rhema is the message spoken; logos is the content of the message; rhema is the communication of that message.

The last three chapters make an already good work a great work in dealing with the will of purpose, the will of desire, and the will of permission. I commend this volume to you without reservation.

Jack Taylor

Introduction

One of the most difficult tasks, by the consensus of most Christians, is how to determine the will of God. The greatest desire, it seems, is to know God's will. Christians often comment, "If only God had written some word regarding my decision, my problem, or my need." Most people would like a specific word, yet God has not given us just one, but many Scriptures on how to discover His will. If we have a problem, it is: we don't want to spend the time discovering His will for anything in our lives. Impatience is the sin of our times. We are always in a hurry. We want ready-made decisions yesterday. We don't want to work at discovering what God thinks or wants. Popular thinking comments, "Go for broke. Make the decision now. Fifty percent of the time you'll likely be right." But there is not a shortcut for the impatient or the lethargic. Every chapter in this book reveals methods which will require prayer, time, and effort, as well as commitment. Paul expressed this commitment well:

> I beseech you therefore, brethren, by the mercies of God, that ye present your bodies a living sacrifice, holy, acceptable unto God, which is your reasonable service. And be not conformed to this world: but be ye trans-

formed by the renewing of your mind, that ye may prove what is that good, and acceptable, and perfect will of God. (Rom. 12:1-2).

God constantly made known His will to the people of the Bible. Some listened and obeyed; some never heard His explicit will because they never obeyed His will as stated in the commands of His word from His messengers. It is obvious that God was delighted when His followers did His will. And the more one obeyed God's will, the more of His will God revealed.

God was very minute and detailed in the giving of that will. This can be verified by the fact that He gave us sixty-six books in His Bible with details as to His desires for our lives. I can say, with authority, that God wants to reveal His will to us.

One person noted that we parents don't tell our children to obey us or else be disciplined, and then fail to tell them what to do. That practice is foolishness. And God is not foolish. He wants us to obey His will; thus, He must want us to know it. And if He wants us to know His will so we can obey it, then He must be willing to give it to us in understandable ways.

God does not give us a Bible and demand that we live by it the best we can, but He also gives the Holy Spirit to guide us into all truth. Then if we do not obey the Word, He will expect us to be ready to give an accounting. If we are to give an accounting for the decisions that we make, then it must be assumed that God is going to become involved in the decision-making process (Rom. 14:12). Certainly He expects those of us who seek His will to live within His moral commands. "If I regard iniquity in my heart, the Lord will not hear me" (Ps. 66:18).

God is interested in the day-by-day or ordinary decisions of life. This is the reason He grants wisdom to the ones asking (see chapter 1). God wants to be involved in our decision-making processes. *And the person who truly wants to know and to follow the will of God can do so, for it is difficult to get outside of God's will when one's life is committed to doing that will.*

Just because many people have misused the processes in determining the will of God does not mean that there is no plan of God for our lives or no preference of God in our nonmoral decisions. The phrase "God told me" can be glibly used by the novice, but such use does not mean that God has spoken to that person about anything. Misuse of a principle or method is no reason to abandon it. Immaturity is immaturity regardless of where one finds it. Some writers on the will of God continually use examples of immature people when they discuss the traditional view of an individual will, but they always use a mature person when referring to their proposed view.

Obviously, most people live as though God were not concerned about their day-to-day decisions. They do not take time to check in with the indwelling Holy Spirit. Thus, any book that gives people the freedom to make decisions without checking in with the Holy Spirit will be accepted readily. Even though some books on the will of God contain many correct principles, these books *usually contain some* incorrect ones as well. These authors often do not see the necessity of the traditional "call" into special Christian service. They often misinterpret the traditional view regarding God's best in marriage by saying a marriage is doomed if one marries the wrong person. Their wrong conclusions are made because they maintain that the traditional view advocates that such a couple can never experience God's blessing. Many such marriages have proved that God does bless when the couple yields to Him.

God is concerned about every area of life, major or minor. Our responsibility is to be available to God for all things and for all decisions. God meets us where we are. And whatever it takes for God to meet us on a personal level, He will do so. For this reason, God has given to every believer the Holy Spirit. He has been given to us to convict us, to indwell us, to magnify Jesus in us, to guide us into truth, to give us His guidance and to give impressions within our inner spirits. "The Spirit itself [Himself][1] beareth witness with our spirit, that we are the children of God" (Rom. 8:16).

The Bible has been given to enable us to learn God's sovereign will as well as His moral will, but it also has been given to us for examples regarding His guidance.

> Now these things were our examples, to the intent we should not lust after evil things, as they also lusted.
> Now all these things happened unto them for ensamples: and they are written for our admonition, upon whom the ends of the world are come (1 Cor. 10:6,11).

Many of the Bible examples relate to God's guidance of His people; they show how God gave directions and how the people obeyed or disobeyed. How can they be examples to us if they are not to give us guidelines in determining the will of God? Every teacher and proclaimer of the Word knows the need of the hearers for biblical concepts in every area of life. Thus, a search is conducted for these concepts so as to give guidance to the people. "All scripture is given by inspiration of God, and is profitable for doctrine, for reproof, for correction, for instruction in righteousness: That the man of God may be perfect, throughly furnished unto all good works" (2 Tim. 3:16-17). To say that examples from the past are not applicable today is to deny the proper exegesis of the passages in the Corinthian letter. The Holy Spirit who indwells us can give guidance to us just as He did to the Old and New Testament people. To believe otherwise is to deny the value of their examples.

Some writers also try to rule out God's willingness to give us divine guidance in our decision making by the selection of a few verses that seem to indicate that the apostolic people, when making their decisions, thought a matter through without the leadership of the Holy Spirit. But conclusions must not be derived on what is not said in a few verses, especially when divine leadership is evident in so many other Scriptures. Committed Christians are not left to their choices and spiritual expediency. We have a God who loves us and cares for us and is willing to assist in every area of our lives. God is interested in us and thinks of us often. "If I should count them, they are more in number than the sand: when I awake, I am still with thee" (Ps. 139:18). Since God is interested in us, then He must be willing to reveal to us what His choice or preference is in any matter we face.

In the "wisdom view" of ascertaining the will of God in nonmoral areas, we are told to use our minds, to trust God for guidance in the decision-making process, and to submit to the sovereign leadership of God in our lives. Proponents of the wisdom view contend that God does not have a specific will for Christians in nonmoral decisions. If they mean God does not have a specific will whether we eat chicken or fish for dinner, I can agree. But if they mean

God has no interest or preference in the decisions regarding a person's calling, vocation, marriage, home life, and so forth, then I must disagree.

A person's choice of a mate is important. It is not "Lord any." That would be like the letter a teenaged boy wrote to his girl friend named "Amy" Lou. He addressed the envelope "Any" Lou. Laughingly, his brothers and sisters told him that he must have been desperate since "any" Lou would be all right for him. Judging from the bad marriages of some today, any person would have been a suitable spouse.

The concept of an individual will is not to be considered as a dot as some writers contend. I do not believe that God's individual will covers every little detail of life regarding which clothes to wear, which food to choose from a menu, or which shoe to put on first. God expects us to be above the ridiculous. But I do believe that God is willing to reveal His will in every important decision we face. A person can get help from God regarding nonmoral decisions. If God does leave to us, as some say, freedom of choice in the nonmoral areas, can we exercise that freedom to check in with God to see what His choice is in any decision we face? We can exercise this freedom.

This book is not an attempt to discuss or to refute all the differing ways of determining the will of God. Rather, it is an effort to provide ways and means for a committed Christian to discover God's will of desire in any area of concern. God's willingness to be involved totally in our lives through the indwelling Holy Spirit makes it mandatory that He be involved in our decision making, too.

The first eight chapters of this book deal with practical ways to determine or to know the will of God. These are biblical ways, but they are tested ways as well. Many have sought the will of God by means of one of these methods and have not only discovered God's will but have found peace in the doing of that will. The ninth chapter reveals another way to discover the will of God, but one must wait for supernatural guidance.

There is progression in these methods. One who wants additional confirmation may continue to move from one method of discovering God's will to another to confirm the first divine impression.

Wanting to be certain is never wrong, but it is wrong to doubt God when His will is revealed. It is not doubt to want a confirmation of God's will that involves a lifetime commitment or obligation or a serious need. God is ready not just to reveal His will; He is fully as ready to confirm that revealed will.

The application of the principles here will not only enable you to discover God's will but will help to confirm it and bring peace to your heart and life.

Too often people claim that problems and tragedies which they do not understand are the will of God. It seems that most people feel they have to express themselves under tragic conditions, and not knowing what to say, they drop in the "magic" words: "It's the will of God." Silence often would be the best response to a situation involving tragedy, but too many people seek to fill the air with their "worthwhile stuff," even though it may be biblically incorrect.

There is no comfort in saying to a mother whose child has just been killed by an angry father, "It's the will of God." To her that statement could mean that God either planned such a tragic death, or else He desired it. Also, that statement could mean to her that things on earth were out of God's control. This expression might mean that either God does not know or He does not care, or maybe He knew and cared, but He couldn't do anything about the situation. To say the least, all of these thoughts would be wrong. But if one could plant the thought that God permitted the tragic event without causing it, then comfort could come, especially in light of Romans 8:28, "And we know that all things [good or bad] work together for good to them that love God, to them who are the called according to his purpose."[2]

We hear much today regarding God's sovereignty, which is similar to or the same as God's will of purpose. When people take this biblical doctrine to the extreme, they will finally arrive at the unacceptable doctrine of "what is to be will be." But the conclusion that God determines everything that happens is incorrect, because that view does not take into consideration God's will of desire or permission. It is true that within His sovereignty there is His will of desire or moral will. If there is not a difference, then all people will be saved, and salvation of all (universalism) is not the teaching of the Scriptures. God is not willing (desiring) that any should perish but that all should come to repentance (see chapter 11; also 1 Pet. 3:9).

A study[3] was made of the Greek words in the Bible relating to the will of God from an etymological (word origin) viewpoint and from their contextual usage. A thorough examination was made of each word in the context of the Scriptures. The results of the study are found in this book, especially in the last three chapters. These chapters give the theological basis of determining the will of God, for it is so easy to pass off that which we do not understand in life as "the will of God." A study of the will of God makes an informed person want to ask in those situations, "Which will of God: the will of purpose, or the will of desire, or the will of permission?" They are all different.

In Matthew 1:19 the text reads: "And Joseph her husband, being a righteous man, and not willing to make her a public example, was minded to put her away privily" (ASV). In the context it is recorded that Mary was with the child of the Holy Spirit before she and Joseph came together. Joseph was confronted with a difficult decision. There were two courses open to him. Either he could charge Mary with adultery and thus make her a public example and let the law take its course, or he could divorce her privately without any publicity. In this deliberation there were two motives that led Joseph in his resolve: one was his being a righteous man, and the other was his being unwilling to make Mary a public example. Joseph resolved on the milder course of divorcing her. The verb *minded* means that he came to this decision after deliberation while the verb *willing* denotes only the desire or wish that prompted him.

Therefore, "willing" denotes "inclination in general," and "minded" indicates a "deliberate decision" between different courses of action. Thus, we can see there is a *will of desire* and a *will of purpose* as based upon deliberation.

The *permissive will* of God takes into consideration the awareness of God regarding a situation He permits or allows without interference on His part. He permits the event to come to pass according to the laws of nature or according to Satan's interference.

A reading of this book's last three chapters, which contain a detailed study of the Scriptures and comments, enables us to understand God's will from His perspective and also to minister to the victims of tragedy in a more intelligent and compassionate manner. These chapters will also give us a biblical base for the discovery of the will of God for our lives.

Debating the merits of the methods will be a waste of time, but plunging into a search for the will of God in some area of our lives will prove rewarding and satisfying. Once we are caught up in discovering God's will, we will continue to walk with God and find exhilarating excitement in that walk.

1

Receiving Divine Impressions

A young preacher had prayed, along with several friends, that the Lord might give him a dedicated Christian wife. In fact, he "claimed" a wife by faith and believed the Lord would lead him to the right young woman. Later, when he was in a revival meeting, he saw a young woman sitting on the front row in the church auditorium; it was obvious she loved the Lord, and the Lord gave him a deep impression that she was "the one." The verification that the impression was a divine one came when, after a period of dating, the young woman agreed to marry him.[1]

Decisions of this nature could be the rule and not the exception. But this type of decision is the exception because people don't know how to make a right decision or don't want to spend the time doing so.

Once a person is saved, God wants that person to operate out of his/her inner spirit where the Holy Spirit dwells. And the Spirit is in a person to enable him to do what God commands him from His Word, for it is in the Word that we find what God commands and wants. The Holy Spirit resides in believers to help them in their praying, giving, and decision making. And a person can be assured of making right decisions if he will follow the divine impressions that come from the Lord.

All kinds of decisions are faced in the day-by-day process of living. Everyone needs to start the day by asking for wisdom for the many decisions of that day. These day-by-day decisions can be made by divine impressions one receives from the Lord.

People often become impatient. They want the answer immediately. Often two people may be caught in one section of a revolving door because one simply could not wait. Life is one big hurry, hurry. A person of this nature probably won't have time to apply the principles presented in this book.

Believers are indwelt, enabled, and enlightened by the Holy Spirit and are given divine impressions by Him. The will of God may be known through these divine impressions.[2] Making right decisions is important to every one of us who are followers of Jesus Christ. Divine impressions are the Holy Spirit's specialty, and with such impressions we can make right decisions and correct choices in our daily walk with the Lord. The pertinent question at this point is: "How may we receive divine impressions?"

James, the half brother of Jesus, said, "But let patience have her perfect work, that ye may be perfect and entire, wanting nothing. If any of you lack wisdom, let him ask of God, that giveth to all men liberally, and unbraideth not; and it shall be given him. But let him ask in faith, nothing wavering" (1:4-6). In this passage James is giving instructions on how to receive wisdom for the trials that a Christian faces. But it is my belief that this same method of receiving wisdom for trials can be used to receive divine impressions for the decisions of life. So, in this passage six steps are set forth to help us receive divine impressions so we can make right decisions. These steps may be found not only in James but in other Scriptures as well.

When these steps are studied and applied in our daily walk with the Lord, then we will make fewer incorrect decisions in our lives and more right ones.

Acknowledge Our Sins

Acknowledging our sins means to keep confession of our sins up-to-date. There are many, many big sins that must go, and too many of these will not go easily; but big sins are usually not the problem. The problem of confession involves the "little sins," as we call them, such as being jealous, envious, resentful, critical, worried. However, God views these sins as big ones which can really cut off what God is wanting to do in our lives. When we become involved in a big problem or trial, we have self-pity in life, self-promotion in work, or self-indulgence in our spare time. We are not sensitive to the Spirit; we are not sensitive to one another; we are touchy; we are resentful; we are defensive. And all of these "little" things can keep us defeated.

God declares, according to 1 John 1:9, that we must confess our sins, and we must keep them confessed. Every time the Holy Spirit reveals that something is wrong in our lives, we must confess it. It is doubtful that the Lord wants us to come and say, "Now, Lord, you know all of my sins; I confess all of them to you." He wants us to be *definite* about them. He says that being a "little" sharp with our companion or having a "little" pride is not acceptable. We must confess these sins to the Lord and to our companion. Sometimes parents make mistakes in dealing with their children; the parents become unjustly angry, and the children know it. Therefore, these parents must confess to the children that they have become angry if the children are going to accept their parents for being honest Christians.

Satan will tell us many times that if we confess any type of a sin to anybody, then that person will think less of us. He insinuates that our children won't think much of us, our companions won't think much of us, our pastor won't think much of us, and our church won't think much of us. That's how the devil keeps us from being definite and honest about our own sins. Then we miss the blessing, and others miss the blessing, too. God wants us to become willing to get our sins out in the open. When we tell the Holy Spirit who indwells us to take over our lives, He'll take over until we cease to obey the word. Therefore, we must keep our sins confessed up to date.

Allow the Holy Spirit to Be in Control

If we take James 1:5 and don't add to it the total teaching of the Bible, we may find ourselves in trouble. In Ephesians 5:18, Paul said, "Be filled with the Spirit." The Holy Spirit needs to control us, to point out our sins and our failures, and to zero in on the right decisions. He is not negative. He is only negative to the degree that we make Him negative, and that is when we sin. When we arrive at the point where we can be without sin for a period of time, the Spirit has an opportunity to be positive in our lives. A person should come to the place where he can live without sins . . . in between sins. God doesn't want us to be continually sinning. Sins may occur occasionally, but there should be some time in between our sins. Our living without habitually sinning is what God expects and wants, and this is what God calls the life of holiness. When we learn how to keep confession up-to-date, there should be a time in our lives when we do not sin. This time may be a short—five minutes, or maybe an hour, or maybe a day or longer. When this time without sin occurs, the Holy Spirit will not leave us alone. He will empower us for all we do for the Lord and will give divine directions for our lives.[3]

Admit the Need of Wisdom

"If any of you lack wisdom, . . ." James said. This phrase means for us to admit that we need wisdom. What is wisdom? It is the ability to see things from God's point of view. Everyone should want to see things from God's point of view. Paul said, "We are asking God that you may see things, as it were, from his point of view by being given spiritual insight and understanding" (Col. 1:9, Phillips). "Entire" means "full" and "wanting nothing" as James said (1:4) God wants all of us to reach maturity and to have fullness, wanting nothing. Maturity is God's goal for every believer. We will never see things from God's point of view until we study the Bible. First, let's admit our need of the ability to see things from God's point of view.

Wisdom is also the ability to make right choices. When we lack the ability to make right choices, we should admit it. The word *wisdom* also means to have discernment, sensitivity, or practical insight. God wants to give wisdom to us. In James 1:5 He, in effect, was saying "All you have to do is admit you need wisdom" (author's paraphrase).

Often the rich and intellectual do not believe that they need anything from God. These people are living a selfish kind of life and are attempting to lift themselves by their own bootstraps. And, suddenly one day, it's all going to come to nought. Watergate is a classic example. Some of the most intelligent men in all the world were involved in the Watergate scandal. Their intellect has amazed those who have listened to them through these years, especially Charles Colson, who has written three books on his experiences. These men were operating out of their intellect.

Much of this country is being directed in Washington or in the state capitols from the intellectual viewpoint only. Training, studying, and going to school are absolutes. But these activities are not enough. It takes the Holy Spirit to enlighten the intellect, so a person may make correct decisions. Too often, the people in Washington and in the state capitols have not had divine wisdom—and they desperately need it. One of their biggest problems is that they aren't willing to admit they need wisdom. This admission is difficult for preachers, staff members, and born-again Christians. These, too, have difficulty admitting a need. Failing to make decisions based upon the Spirit is the source of most problems in many churches. Pride is a sin that keeps us from admitting our lack of wisdom. It requires hungry people to admit the need for wisdom, but those people are the satisfied ones at the end of the search.

Ask for Wisdom

James wrote, "If any of you lack wisdom," ask for it. Speak up and ask for it. Asking is so simple. James on another occasion penned this phrase, "Ye have not, because ye ask not" (4:2). Most of us will not admit our need, and others merely do not ask. Ask.

Wisdom is not given by moaning, groaning, or working ourselves up into a high level of believing, and while we're at the high peak of believing, then asking God for what we want before our faith diminishes. We're tempted to do that. Too often we want to pump up our muscles of faith so we can ask God quickly and hope He will immediately give the answer before we become cowardly with the faith we have. Asking God for something quickly while we have the faith is not what God wants. He wants us to come to Him in honest prayer.

We are to ask for wisdom in faith (1:6). Faith may be seen between almost every word in verse 5. To ask God for something without believing that He will give it is fruitless. When we ask God for something, we must ask in prayer, and we must ask for it in faith. We must believe that He will respond. Faith must be the kind that is without fear. Faith removes fear. "Fear knocked at the door; faith answered, and nobody was there."

James meant that we don't have to worry about God calling us "dummies" every time we come to Him. Some people alibi, "Oh, we mustn't go to God very often, for God will get the impression that we don't know anything." It is true; we don't know much or have anything that has not been given to us by the Lord. When we finally get to the point of being bankrupt and desperate, we are in business with God. When we come to feel that we have nothing, that we need God, and if God doesn't come through we are "sunk," then we are in business. So what God really says is that He is not going to upbraid us or call us dummies. He's not going to come back at us and say, "I'm tired of hearing from you." God delights when we come to Him.

No one is to fear that God will be too elusive to give wisdom. Some feel that God's gift of wisdom is something about which we can't talk to any human being. We need not worry about that. If it is of any concern to our hearts, then God is interested, too.

This faith must be one that refuses to doubt. We must not doubt. People who doubt will not receive what they request. Doubting excludes wisdom and many other blessings from the Lord. No one can come to the Lord and say, "Now, Lord, I'm here; I'm one of Your children down here on earth. You know me real well, *for* I'm always coming to You. I'm just not sure You are going to do anything for me this time, but I'd like to tell You what I need anyway." God may hear the first part of the prayer, but we must not tell God that we're not sure He's going to answer. We must come to God and say, "God, You said, 'Come to Me boldly,' and here I am. And You said, 'If you will ask for wisdom, I'll give it'; therefore, I am accepting it."

Adore God for Giving Wisdom

We should thank the Lord for the wisdom even though we do not have it. He promised that He would give if we asked. Notice the basis for that asking: "It shall be given" (Jas. 1:5). This verse states that if we have admitted that we need wisdom, that is, the ability to make the right choice, and have asked for that ability, then God has given it. So somewhere between the asking and the receiving God has given wisdom, and we ought to thank Him. You reply, "But I don't have it in my hand." That doesn't matter; He has already given wisdom. He said He has given it. We are to thank Him before we receive this wisdom. If we haven't thanked God very much, then we need to do so. We can look to God and ask Him for something, and then thank Him for giving it to us even before we have received it! We must believe that we already have that which was requested before we receive it in order to have it! As someone commented, "Act like it is so, even though it is not so, so that it will be so." That is faith. Right here is where you exercise your faith. Let us exercise our faith by thanking God for the wisdom before we receive it and believe that God is in the process of giving it to us.

Doubt means that we don't believe God will give what we asked for in the first place. Prayer is not hoping and guessing; it is believing and receiving. Notice what James said in verse 5, He gives "to all men." The word *men* is not in the original (It is in italics in the King James translation). So God gives to all. He gives to all who believe and trust and ask. *Nobody is left out.* God is going to give. And then He says that He not only gives to all but gives *liberally.* He gives more than we ask for. That's the kind of God we have. If we are willing to come to Him and simply admit we have a need and ask for it, the Bible says He gives to every one, and He gives an abundant supply. Therefore, we should start adoring Him and thanking Him right now.

Apply the Divine Impressions

Let us keep in step with the Spirit, for He's the one who gives this wisdom (Gal. 5:25). Let us also move out and act upon the divine impressions that follow. If we have followed the directions in gaining wisdom, then we can follow the next impression that comes to our hearts. We can accept this impression as being from God and follow through accordingly.

It is easy to become confused at this juncture. A divine impression comes into our hearts and we have peace about it, but we hesitate to move on. Hesitation is also a form of doubt. Hesitation, too, must go. This is the place where we ask God for courage to move on in the direction that He has given us.

In applying the divine impression, we must leave to the Holy Spirit the right to block us if we are headed in the wrong direction. By way of illustration, we ask God for wisdom about a job decision, and we thank Him for giving us the ability to make the right choice. And now an impression comes. We have to accept this impression as a divine impression, and once we have accepted it, we act upon it. We follow through, and we leave to the Holy Spirit the right to place before us a roadblock if the decision is wrong for us. Occasionally, we may miss the divine impression, but God doesn't want us to go back over the process repeatedly because that, too, is a sign of doubt. Allowing the Holy Spirit to do some work in our lives means if it is the wrong move, then we let Him close the door.

A young woman dating a young man who is not what he ought to be should not tell God to stop the friend from coming over if he is not right for her. Remember that God is not in the business of taking from us. He is in the business of accepting from us. What she needs to do is give that person to the Lord. And giving is the difference. It is easy to cop-out and come to God, saying, "God, I want to marry this young man, and he looks all right to me, but if he is not all right with You, You keep him from marrying me." Such a statement is not what God wants. He says, "Give that young man to me." If God wants to give him back to you, fine; if not, he'll give you someone else.

We need to look at buying a house in the same manner. We must not say, "God, I'd like to have this house. If it is not the house you want me to have, then you cause that

man not to show up at my house at 2:00 this afternoon."
This prayer is merely a cop-out. What God wants us to do
is to ask Him for a divine impression, and when the divine
impression comes, we proceed. If the house is the wrong
one to buy, let the Holy Spirit stop the purchase. In buying houses, many things can cause a loan not to be ap-
proved. So, we let the Holy Spirit cut off the purchase, and
when He does cut it off, we don't ask what's wrong with
our walk with God. We just go back to the Word and
repeat the same process.

Acting upon the impression means doing what we think
is best in the face of a given situation. This acting upon the
impression indicates that we believe a certain action is the
best thing to do. Sometimes we think God has a different
approach. During a television program, which was one of
those guessing games, a fellow was trying to guess which
cities were the farthest apart—New York and London or
New York and Los Angeles. Thinking it was a trick question, he guessed it was farther between New York and Los
Angeles, but he was wrong. And, most likely, his first
impression was that London is farther, but he didn't make
his guess on that impression. *So often we miss the will of
God because we assume what we think is best may not be
the best.* Even though the divine impression came and
coincided with what we thought, we had difficulty with it.

We must trust that the impression is a divine impression
operating through us. Acting upon that divine impression
may coincide with what we have felt all along. So we are
simply trusting that the impression is of divine origin as
it operates through us. Then, let us move out on the as-
sumption that what seems good to us seems good to the
Holy Spirit.

One growing Christian woman who, by her own admission, acted too often upon impulse, felt divinely impressed to quit her public job and to stay at home. She felt that she must be willing to give up possessions and comfort, if need be, and take the step of faith, knowing God would provide. So she shared her heart with her husband. He had no objections but requested that she wait before she acted, so she would be certain she was not acting on impulse instead of impression. Soon it was evident that her impression was right. The place of business where she worked was sold. The new owners' life-styles were unacceptable to her because of her Christian principles: one was involved in astrology, and the other was living out of wedlock with her boyfriend. Being thus assured, she turned in her resignation. Peace came, and peace has continued to be hers in her growth in the Lord.[4]

In summary, let us not spend too much time in rechecking once the divine impression has come. Allow the Holy Spirit to do the blocking. Keep moving. And read on.

2

Claiming the Promises

In my previous book, *The Church in a Storm,* I describe how God broke me in the altar of Leawood.[1] Demonic forces immediately attacked me and continued their attack upon me. The demonic powers whispered that I should be embarrassed and that the people would be ashamed of me, and so forth. So the next morning in my quiet time, I took the harrassment to the Lord in His word. If God wanted to say something, fine. If He chose not to say anything, fine. I would wait on the Lord. I started reading in Isaiah 40.[2] When I came to chapter 49 and had read through most of it, verse 23 leaped from the page to my heart to assure me that God was in control. The last phrase said, "for they shall not be ashamed that wait for me." There was no reason to be embarrassed, so said my Lord. What comfort! What assurance!

Does God speak messages of assurance, comfort, and guidance to us from His Word? Every Bible reader understands the joy of reading the Word of God. But directions for daily decisions can also be found in the Word, if one is willing to consult the Word of God in prayer and faith, is willing to receive an answer or denial of a request, or to receive a confirmation or repudiation of an impression. Even though we may have received an impression through prayer (see chapter 1), the decision may be so significant that we want an additional confirmation. It is then that we go to the Word of God for a personal word that we can believe and act upon. For faith is not a leap into the dark: it is a leap into light! "God never calls on you to jump without His promise or without a word from Him."[3]

> We solemnly assure you that as certainly as God is faithful so we have never given you a message meaning "yes" and "no." Jesus Christ, the Son of God, whom Silvanus, Timothy and I have preached to you, is himself no doubtful quantity, he is the divine "Yes." Every promise of God finds its affirmative in him, and through him can be said the final amen, to the glory of God. We owe our position in Christ to this God of positive promise: it is he who has consecrated us to this special work, he who has given us the living guarantee of the Spirit in our hearts (2 Cor. 1:18-22) Phillips.

Every promise is exactly as God wrote it in His Word. The adage, "God said it, I believe it and that settles it" has too much in it. It should be, "God said it and that settles it, whether I believe it or not."

Our Lord Jesus Christ fulfills every one of God's promises regardless of how many there are. And one of His greatest promises to us as believers is the gift of the Holy Spirit, whose presence in our lives becomes a guarantee that we belong to God and also constitutes the first installment of all that He is going to give us. What a promise! And there are many more for us to claim.

All the promises of God find their guarantee and fulfilment in Jesus Christ. His incarnation, life, death, and resurrection affirmed every promise made about Him and

by Him and guaranteed that the God who brought fulfilment of His promises in Jesus Christ is the same God who
assures the fulfilment of every promise to us.[4]

When we say "amen," or however we affirm God, in our
services, in our quiet times, or whenever, we affirm that
God is keeping His word through Christ to us and that He
will continue to do so. The New Testament Christians
were known for their "amens." In a few churches, a resounding "amen" can be heard today. Every "amen"
truly declaring that a message has hit the heart undoubtedly brings glory to God.

God's promises live on. They stand. They cannot fail.
These promises work in every area of life. We may have
needs, problems, difficulties to be met, and decisions to be
made. As we read the Bible may we depend upon the
Holy Spirit that He may point out the promises and enable us to claim them. Every page of the blessed Book
may have a promise just for us.

Look for the Promises

One fellow who looked for a verse to ascertain God's
direction in a matter decided he'd just seek a quick answer by taking his Bible, allowing it to fall open and then
blindly placing his finger on a verse. When he did this, he
looked down and read the verse. It said, "Judas went out
and hanged himself." That verse didn't help him very
much; so he tried the same procedure again. This time the
verse said, "Go thou and do likewise." That experience
shook him terribly, but he decided to try one more time.
After all, he thought, *the third time is a charm.* This time
his finger touched the verse which said, "And what thou
doest, do quickly."

Seriously, a person who wants to know the will of God

must not open the Bible anywhere, close his eyes, and
place a finger on a Scripture. Most of the time, if not all
the time, that person will miss the will of God. There is
no substitute for honest, dedicated living and Bible study
when one looks for a word from the Word.

God has spread a table full of promises. Someone has
said there are seven thousand obvious promises in the
Word of God. Some are conditional; others are uncondi-
tional. For instance, "My God shall supply all of your need
according to his riches in glory by Christ Jesus" (Phil.
4:19). "I can do all things through Christ which streng-
theneth me" (Phil. 4:13). ". . . lo, I am with you alway, even
unto the end of the world" (Matt. 28:20). These are obvious promises, and they have been given to all of us. Our
need is to claim these promises, for they are ours. Look for
God's promises, for they are in the Word of God.

Promises are to be discovered. Better expressed, these
promises can be discovered; they can be found. We don't
go to the living room looking for food; instead we go to the
kitchen. We don't go to a magazine or newspaper to find
the promises but to the Word of God. We are so practical
in our daily living, yet so impractical in our Christian
living. Most of us will go and ask a friend, "What do you
think?" And finally we get around to the preacher and
say, "Pastor, what do you think I ought to do?" Then, if
we don't like what the pastor says, we go back around our
circle of friends asking the same thing. We don't have to
do that. We can go to the Word of God and find a promise.

God has given us these obvious promises to help us to
discover many things in our lives. When we find these
obvious promises, we should mark them, meditate on
them, and memorize them. This process involves visualiz-
ing, personalizing, and harmonizing them.

Special promises for special needs and directions may also be found in the Word. Any verse or passage may become a potential directive to our hearts and lives. We must look for these promises in a spirit of prayer and expectancy; they are there. The Holy Spirit is ready to make one of these special promises real to our hearts.

Listen to the Promises

We must listen as we read the Bible. In fact, we read so we can listen. We can't listen to the Bible unless we read it or it is read to us. The word *listen* doesn't mean to look for a promise and then listen for something to come "out of the blue." The word means to listen for the Spirit's whisper to our hearts as we read. Thus, we need to read and reread, listen and keep on listening. God isn't necessarily interested in filling our minds with facts or in satisfying our intellectual curiosity, but He is basically interested in one thing—our obedience. And how are we going to know what to obey if we do not listen?

Biblical principles may be found in most every verse of the Bible if we read and listen to the Word until God literally brings out of the Word a principle to guide us. It is amazing what we will receive when we take the time in our devotions or Bible study to let God reveal His principles to us. "Revelation happens when the Holy Spirit takes the Word of God and so impresses it upon the heart that it becomes as real and personal as if God were speaking audibly."5

Listening is expecting a verse to leap from the pages of the Bible to our hearts as we read the Word. The giving of the verse is the work of the Holy Spirit. He may give a directive, change the directions of our lives, promise to meet a need, give comfort for a sorrow, or say no to a request or desire.

While reading the Bible and listening for a message regarding my vocal chord problems, the Lord gave me a verse. I was unable to use my vocal chords because of an allergy. One morning during my quiet time I was reading the thirty-third chapter of Jeremiah. Regretfully, I must confess I was so concerned about the difficulty with my voice that I also had difficulty in listening. When I had finished the chapter, nothing had come from the verses, but I felt impressed to reread some of the chapter. It was as if God asked, "Why don't you listen as you read?" Then I started again with verse 1, reading and listening. Suddenly verses 3 and 6 became alive to my heart. These were mine. I claimed them.

> Call unto me, and I will answer thee, and show thee great and mighty things, which thou knowest not. . . . Behold, I will bring it health and cure, and I will cure them, and will reveal unto them the abundance of peace and truth (Jeremiah 33:3, 6).

I marked the verses and placed the date in the margin of my Bible. My vocal chords would clear up, and they did, stronger than ever.

Latch on to the Promises

Latching onto a given scriptural promise means to underscore it, date it, and initial it. But this concept involves more. We must accept the promise, claim it, and share it, too. This process is called putting our faith out on a limb. But once we've heard from God, there must be no turning back or backing up.

When the heroes of faith of Hebrews 11 received their

report from God, they were persuaded of it, embraced it, counted it so, and confessed it to be so. And God honored their faith. Having not seen, they saw! What they saw could not be taken from their heart of faith. They believed regardless of the circumstances.

Abraham, the patriarch of the Old Testament, envisioned a nation through his son Isaac. It was such a revelation of God that when God told him to take his son Isaac and sacrifice him on an altar, Abraham was willing to obey. Abraham believed God was able to raise his son from the dead, if necessary, in order to keep His promise (Heb. 11:17-19).

When Manley Beasley[6] got into the presence of God with regard to his three "terminal" illnesses, he knew God's way as he received a word from the Lord. He was reading Psalm 128. The Holy Spirit caused verse 6 to leap from the page of the Bible to his heart and assure him that he too would live and see his children's children. God gave him the definite impression that this was his special promise to claim. That promise is still being fulfilled for him. The psalmist declared that God never forgets His covenant or promises (111:5). God truly establishes us in Christ Jesus (2 Cor. 1:21).

Live by the Promises

E. F. Hallock, longtime pastor of the First Baptist Church of Norman, Oklahoma, probably came nearer to living by the promises than any other person. When he was approaching sixty-five years of age, he faced three major decisions—whether to retire, whether to build, and whether to take a mission trip out of the country. Being a man of God who made it a practice to live daily by the promises, he took all three decisions to the Lord one morning in his quiet time. (I would suggest to a novice not to take more than one request at a time to the Lord. More than one request certainly will not confuse God, but it could confuse you.) For his Bible study time he was reading from Genesis 28. Suddenly verses 13, 14, and 15 leaped from the pages to his heart. Verse 13 confirmed to him that he was not to retire. Verse 14 confirmed that he was to lead the church in building on the west. Verse 15 confirmed that God would bless his mission trip and give him a safe trip. He continued to pastor the church for several years before retiring, led the church to expand on all four sides as promised in verse 14, and completed his mission trip safely.[7]

Once a word has been given, it is time to act upon the revealed promise and to start applying it in our lives. "Having therefore these promises, dearly beloved, let us cleanse ourselves from all filthiness of the flesh and spirit, perfecting holiness in the fear of God" (2 Cor. 7:1). There is to be no display of pride because God has spoken to you from the Word through the Holy Spirit. It is a time of moving on with God and living by faith in the promises of the Word of God.

Since the Holy Spirit is God's first installment gift to us that He will keep all of His promises, we can act on the promise that God has given us in His Word (2 Cor. 1:22). If we have been seeking a word regarding a mate, a college, or a move to another location, then we can take the promise, thank God for it, and start acting accordingly.

Applying the promise to the situation reveals our faith to be genuine. Until we act upon the promise, then all of our reading, finding, and claiming are just mental exercises. Possibly we need to back up and confess the desire of our heart to be so, if we are having problems proceeding with the promise. We may also need to keep on sharing the promise with others. This act of faith in sharing our promise moves God into action. He either has to come through, or else we have to admit that we failed in the process of receiving the promise.

Learn from Missing the Promises

Sometimes we may make a mistake in determining the will of God by this method or even by one of the other methods. We are not infallible. We may just miss the will of God as we search the Scriptures looking for the promise that the Holy Spirit gives to confirm to our spirit a certain direction. Paul missed the Spirit's direction (Acts 16:7). "After they were come to Mysia, they assayed [attempted] to go into Bithynia: but the Spirit suffered [allowed] them not."[8] The true follower of the Lord Jesus can depend on the Holy Spirit to redirect him when necessary. It is better to make a mistake seeking the will of God than to make the same mistake without having sought the will of God at all.

One pastor taught his people that a special word from the Bible is not needed in regard to faith, morals, or doctrine; that special directions for the daily responsibilities of life may be received through our authorities; and that promises from the Bible may be received from the Holy Spirit in regard to our ministry and devotional life. In no way will these promises violate the Bible or the authority and counsel God has placed in our lives.

A pastor had believed God for a staff member.[9] God had confirmed his impression with a promise from the Word about a young man. When the young man was contacted, he prayed and agreed to come. But then his present church offered to raise the young man's salary above the new church's offer; he called the pastor and declined the call. The pastor felt that his promise had failed, but God gave him another word which was 2 Cor. 1:21. Now, who missed the will of God? Time revealed that the young man had missed God's will in turning down the call to the new church as his present church did not keep her financial promises, and he began to move from church to church with short stops at each different situation. So in many instances, it may not be the person who lives by the promises who misses the will of God, especially when other people are involved who do not live by the promises.

"Our mistakes can remind us to approach the scriptures with the primary purpose of knowing God better and learning to see things as he does, so that we can walk in *his* ways."10

> For the Word of God is quick, and powerful, and sharper than any two-edged sword, piercing even to the dividing asunder of soul and spirit, and of the joints and marrow, and is a discerner of the thoughts and intents of the heart (Heb. 4:12).

Lay Aside Misuse of the Promises

People often misuse the promises, and because of their misuse they miss the will of God, mislead many, and cause some not to accept the claiming of the promises as a good method.

Misuse of the promises can take extreme directions. Promises can be used to manipulate people. A special promise is given and then persons are asked to apply the promise in some area of their lives. This suggestion overlooks the principle that revelation by the Spirit is given to the *individual.*

Some misuse the promises in a name-it-and-claim-it game. If they want to be rich, own a new car, or have some other luxury, they are to name-it-and-claim-it, and they will have what they claim. But this method fails, too.

Others take the use of the promises so lightly and look only for a verse to affirm their desires. They do not want God to say no. This error is often caused by a desire for a shortcut to prayer and Bible reading. Instead of using one or more of the tested methods described in this book, they want a magic formula or a spiritual horoscope.

None of us want God to say no, but we know that sometimes He does say no to the honest seeker. I know that God can give a negative response. On more than one occasion, when I have sought a promise from the Word of God about a desire, I have been given an impression to wait on the Lord as noted in Isaiah 40:31 or to remain silent as revealed in Isaiah 41:1. God is going to say no on occasion, and when He does, we should not be surprised but accept His answer.

Those who misuse the promises as found in the Word, and those who react to their misuse, are left without the joy of seeing what God can do and will do through the proper use of His promises. There is direction in the use of promises as well as joy.

3

"Putting Out the Fleece"

A pastor was heard telling another pastor that he had put out the fleece in regard to his church beginning a cooperative work with a church in Japan. He stated that he had put out three things that had to come to pass before his church would be ready. In his sharing with the pastor and with the rest of us seated nearby, he said that two of the three things had come to pass, but he was waiting on the third one before taking action.

"But I thought that putting out the fleece," some say, "was for the Old Testament people only." Every Scripture can be profitable and beneficial to the person who takes seriously knowing and doing the will of God. Paul said the Old Testament stories were written as examples for our instruction. (Study 1 Cor. 1:10:11; Rom. 15:4.)

The use of *fleece* differs with some people. They would have us to believe that the Old Testament examples of guidance provide only examples of supernatural guidance and that they are not the norm in the New Testament and for today. But Paul stated emphatically that the Old Testament stories are examples for us. How could Gideon's "fleece" be an example for us if it was not an example of confirming a divine directive to us? The use of the trivial as fleece (a car running a stop sign or a team winning an athletic event) is insufficient evidence to toss out a method of confirmation of God's directive to us. A person who uses the fleece is not to be a spiritual ignoramus or a constant backslider. God is not interested in confirming His will to such people. But He is interested in confirming His will to spiritual people who are growing in the Lord Jesus Christ.

Putting out the fleece is credited to Gideon as he needed and wanted a confirmation of God's directive to him to go to battle against the Midianites with an assured victory.

> And Gideon said unto God, If thou wilt save Israel by mine hand, as thou hast said, Behold, I will put a fleece of wool in the floor; and if the dew be on the fleece only, and it be dry upon all the earth beside, then shall I know that thou wilt save Israel by mine hand, as thou hast said. And it was so: for he rose up early on the morrow, and thrust the fleece together, and wringed the dew out of the fleece, a bowl full of water. And Gideon said unto God, Let not thine anger be hot against me, and I will speak but this once: let me prove, I pray thee, but this once with the fleece; let it now be dry only upon the fleece, and upon all the ground let there be dew. And God did so that night: for it was dry upon the fleece only, and there was dew on all the ground (Judg. 6:36-40).

Each time Gideon put out the fleece, God gave the answer as requested. All of us would like to be involved in this kind of action, especially if God would give us an obvious answer as He did for Gideon. Then we could move on and make our major decisions easily. A genuine follower of the Lord can put out the fleece for the major decisions of life. But the fleece should be used on a limited basis because it was used infrequently in the Bible.

Abraham's servant, who was sent to Haran to find a wife for Isaac, put out the fleece to make certain that he obtained the wife that God wanted for Isaac. The servant prayed to the Lord God,

> Let it come to pass, that the damsel to whom I shall say, Let down thy pitcher, I pray thee, that I may drink; and she shall say, Drink, and I will give thy camels drink also: let the same be she that thou hast appointed for thy servant Isaac; and thereby shall I know that thou hast shewed kindness unto my master (Gen. 24:14).

And Rebekah did exactly as the servant had asked of the Lord God (vs. 18-19). After the servant told Rebekah his request and prayer, she went back with him and became the wife of Isaac (v. 67).

But to put out the fleece, one must be willing to be what Gideon was and to do what Gideon did. Too often when people hear about putting out the fleece, they are ready to use this method without paying the price. To put out the fleece without paying the price would be like Jesus wanting to be the Savior without being willing to die on the cross, like Paul wanting to be a missionary without being willing to suffer the hardships, or like a young man wanting to be a preacher without being willing to prepare.

An older man felt the call of God to the ministry. As a result of that call, he wanted a verification. So one day he asked God to verify that he was called to the ministry by allowing a bird to fly into the church through an open window and to light on the pulpit. (This was in the day when air conditioning was not used in churches.) Now that is putting out the fleece. But that man who asked for the bird to fly through the window received the verification of his call at his ordination when a bird flew in and stopped on the pulpit where the preacher was standing.[1]

A study of chapters 6 and 7 in the Book of Judges will reveal the steps necessary to confirm a directive from God or to find the will of God by putting out the fleece.

Major on the Prerequisites

If there is a problem in using this method of determining the will of God, it is in the area of the prerequisites. We are ready to major on putting out the fleece, but we don't want to hear anything about the kind of life required to put out the fleece.

Gideon had already majored on the prerequisites. This does not mean that years before he had sat down and determined what God would expect of him if ever he wanted to put out the fleece. Gideon had simply lived his life in surrender to the living God. He had kept in contact with God. He had lived the right kind of life. He was ready. Since God had communicated His message with him, Gideon undoubtedly felt that he could continue this communication. After all, if the line were open from God to mankind, the same line had to be open from mankind to God.

Gideon was already living the life that God could and would honor. His character revealed the traits that must be in the life of the person who would put out the fleece. These character traits are most important. Right character is always a major and not a minor requirement.

Spiritual Characteristics

What kind of person is God looking for to use? What kind of character must we have if we are to put out the fleece? We do not have to guess. God sent an angel to

Gideon to give His message. And we have the message recorded in the Word of God.

If we are to put out the fleece, we must have a courageous heart, one that is recognizable. God's work takes courage. The angel spoke of Gideon being a "mighty man of valour" (6:12). Courage is determined by one's concept of God. Is God really omnipotent? Is He able to take care of His own? Is He in control of the universe? If we can say yes to these questions, then courage should be ours.

Confidence in God must also be depicted in a person's character and life. Gideon had confidence in God. He knew that God was His source of strength (6:12). If there is no confidence in God, why put out a fleece? The fleece might produce an answer, but we would not know it. We must trust God. Our confidence should be unwavering. When God speaks, He will back up His words with His presence and power. We must believe that God is a rewarder of them who diligently seek Him (Heb. 11:6). Gideon knew that he could talk to God.

> And Gideon said unto him, Oh my Lord, if the Lord be with us, why then is all this befallen us? and where be all his miracles which our fathers told us of, saying, Did not the Lord bring us up from Egypt? but now the Lord hath forsaken us, and delivered us into the hands of the Midianites (Judg. 6:13).

His talk could be considered a little arrogant. But arrogance is not a part of a humble person. Confidence in God is evident when a person can talk with boldness to God in prayer.

An unassumed humility must be evident. Even though we are told to humble ourselves, we cannot call ourselves humble. Humility will express itself. When the angel said all that he had to say to Gideon and bragged on him, Gideon responded, "My family is poor . . . and I am the least in my father's house" (6:15). Instead of claiming to be somebody who was worthy of such praise, Gideon admitted that he was really a nobody. In the Christian life, ability is not what counts but availability. Certainly, God knew of his humility before Gideon said anything, and Gideon may not have had as much natural ability as many other people. However, Gideon was available. And availability brings us into the position where God can and will confirm His will to us through the means of a fleece.

Paul emphasized that God uses the humble folk who just believe God regardless of what takes place (1 Cor. 2—3). These are the kind of folk that God uses and speaks to, and with whom He trusts His will and way.

Reverence of God is another trait demanded of us. Gideon had a holy respect for God. When Gideon perceived that he had seen an angel of the Lord, he said, "Alas, O Lord God! for because I have seen an angel of the Lord face to face" (6:22). Before he could say another word, God broke into his speech and said, "Peace be unto thee; fear not: thou shalt not die" (6:23). Then Gideon built an altar to worship the Lord.

We must reverence God and totally commit ourselves to Him and to His decision in whatever we face. If God is to commit Himself to us, we must commit ourselves to Him (John 2:23-24). Such commitment will lead to worship and praise.

The Spirit of God must anoint those who would put out the fleece. Gideon was anointed by "the Spirit of God" (6:34). The anointing occured just prior to his placing the fleece. But we have had the Spirit of God upon us since our conversion (1 Cor. 12:13). He will not leave us nor forsake us. He is ready to guide us in finding the will of God in any situation. Being Spirit filled is a must if we are to know God's will.

Divine Directives

There must be a divine directive. God gave Gideon a divine directive. "And the Lord said unto him, Surely I will be with thee, and thou shalt smite the Midianites as one man" (6:16). (See 6:14.) If we're going to put out the fleece, our character must be right, and the directive must have already been received from the Lord. At least we should be conscious of a directive from the Lord even though we may be having trouble with God's specific instruction. The fleece comes after we have received our directions from the Lord. Gideon had received his directions but was not yet willing to go because it appeared to be an impossible task. Maybe that's what we need to understand: the fleece may be put out after God has given us a divine directive to do something that looks to be impossible from our viewpoint but is possible only through the power of God.

There are areas in the church in which we move only when God truly gives a directive to move, such as building or relocating. And there are times when we personally just want to know before venturing forth: "Is this the direction that God really wants us to go?" Just as in the church, Christian business persons may want to know God's will before expanding their businesses. Young adults may need a verification of a call into the service of the Lord. God is ready to verify His will to any who will take the time to come to Him.

Maximize the Placing of the Fleece

When we maximize something, we assign the maximum importance to it. To assign the maximum importance to the placing of the fleece, we must put out the fleece in such a way that we can know when God gives an answer. We must not complicate the placing of the fleece. We must not ask God to give two or three answers. When we put out the fleece, we need to make the placing of the fleece definite enough that we will know and not be confused. Remember, we are not going to confuse God, but we may confuse ourselves by complicating the placing of the fleece. Gideon's placing of the fleece here is not complicated. He just said, "Lord, let the dew be on the fleece and let everything be dry around it."[2] That request is definite and concise. One could have known if one had seen the fleece the next morning. Notice also that Gideon decided that he needed another word, and he asked God the second time, "Would You, Lord, let me now ask You to make the fleece dry and everything around it wet with dew?"[3] Here Gideon was not showing doubt so much as he was wanting to be certain. And we have a right to want to be certain, too.

The fleece must be placed in such a way that others may know, too. It is not necessary that others be there, but when we share our story about putting out the fleece and God's answer, it must make sense to them and not be confusing to them. Gideon's experience occurred many, many years ago, but it is still understandable. We understand what Gideon did. Others must understand what we do when we put out the fleece.

Magnify the Results

The word *magnify* means to increase in significance. The results of putting out the fleece can be and must be seen in all their significance. Every detail must be emphasized.

Putting out the fleece is not complete until the results are in. In the midst of the results, God often gives additional instructions. He gave Gideon some instructions that had to be fulfilled if His presence was to be experienced and victory was to be won.

Magnifying the results involves accepting God's answers. If God says no, then a sense of peace ought to pervade the heart as well as a desire to discover what God may want to do about the situation. If God says yes, then we continue to go on with Him.

In each instance of putting out the fleece, God gave a positive answer. Gideon could depend upon God to give the victory over the enemy.

Results also verify the presence of God. The promise that God made to Gideon that He would be with him (6:12,16) was confirmed. God was with him. He would continue to be with Gideon. Whenever God sends us on an errand, He promises to be with us. The task may appear to be impossible to us, but to God nothing is impossible.

The increase in significance of the results involves obedience of the instructions. Gideon had obeyed God. There was no stopping place now. God's instructions had to be obeyed. Gideon was morally bound to obey and so are we.

Before victory could come to Gideon and his people, the army of thirty-two thousand had to be reduced to three hundred. Gideon's army had to be reduced to practically nothing. God said to him, "The people that are with thee are too many for me to give the Midianites into their hands, lest Israel vaunt themselves against me, saying, Mine own hand hath saved me" (7:2). God is saying that the Israelites will brag and claim that they conquered the Midianites when He defeats them. We must not claim God's victories as ours. He will not share His glory.

Obeying the Lord means that we do exactly what God wants, even as He details it. Gideon had not conquered the Midianites just by reducing the army to three hundred. There were other instructions that had to be obeyed. The army had to be equipped with pitchers, candles, and trumpets. When they were equipped with their unusual instruments of war, God told Gideon to order his small army to surround the Midianites and do as they were commanded (7:19-20). When they obeyed, the Midianites fell into the hands of Gideon and his army (7:21-23). The victory was theirs, but God had given it.

Even though we want to put out the fleece, we must not put it out unless we plan to obey God. He will not let us off easily if He shows us His will. Since He knows our hearts, it is doubtful that He would even make His will known to us if He knows that we are not going to follow through with His instructions.

God demands obedience to every command that He gives and verifies. Disobedience is out of the question. Even partial obedience is not the obedience that God demands.

Moses discovered that partial obedience is not satisfactory to God. When Moses and the children of Israel came into the desert of Zin, no water could be found. So the people complained to Moses. He took their need to the

Lord. Thus, the Lord told Moses, "Take the rod, . . . and speak ye unto the rock before their eyes; and it shall give forth his water." But Moses made the mistake of using the rod to strike the rock twice instead of speaking to the rock. Then God revealed to Moses that Moses would not be the one to bring the people of Israel into the land which He had given them (Num. 20:1-12).

Following through with every detail of God's instructions on our part is expected by the Lord and ought to be the desire of every follower. No one has any right to change God's commands to His liking. It is total obedience that God expects when He confirms His will to us in such manner.

People are still putting out the fleece today, and God is still revealing and confirming His will.

One woman who was able and ready to retire from her important job in a department store planned to do so at the end of the year. But when she did not have peace about retiring and when her son said to her that God needed more of His children out in the working world, she seriously sought God's guidance regarding her retirement. The Lord brought to her attention one of her favorite Scriptures: Proverbs 3:5-6. She had sought God's will after her husband's sudden death and before seeking a job, and He had led her to this place of work where she had the opportunity to witness with her life and words. Then remembering Jesus' prayer of seeking the will of the Father about the cross, and recalling Gideon's experience in Judges 6:36-40 in putting out the fleece, she decided to put out the fleece, too. If the Lord wanted her to continue to work, then He would save someone as a result of her witness and life in her place of work. The next day after she had put out her fleece on Sunday, another worker whose marriage had been helped by her testimony came to her and requested that she pray earnestly for a mutual acquaintance who was unsaved and under conviction. She agreed to pray for him and did so on that Monday afternoon. Then on Tuesday someone tapped her on the shoulder. She turned and saw the young man for whom she had prayed the previous day. His face, though covered with tears, was aglow with God. She knew that he had been saved. And she knew that she also had her answer. She was to continue being God's witness and worker in the department store.[4]

4

Living Like the Lord Jesus

The Lord Jesus Christ always pleased the Father (John 8:29). This means that He knew the will of God and obeyed that will. He fitted His life perfectly into the life of the Heavenly Father, and because He conformed to the life of His Father, He was always able to know the will of the Father.

Often Christ Jesus went aside to pray when He lived bodily on this earth. And when He did, He prayed that He might know perfectly what the Father was doing, so He could carry out the Father's will. Once He prayed in behalf of Lazarus who had died. It was a brief prayer, but a very pointed prayer. In fact, in the prayer He made the statement that He was praying in order that the people around him might hear the prayer and might believe in Him as the Son of God (John 11:41-42). And as He prayed, He thanked the Father for having heard Him. He had already checked in with the Father to see what the Father was doing. When He finished His prayer of thanksgiving, He cried out, "Lazarus, come forth." And Lazarus walked out of the tomb (John 11:43-44). It is not difficult to believe that a dead person could be raised from the grave by Jesus, especially if one has already looked ahead in time and discovered that the Father was raising the body.

Jesus, knowing already what the Father was doing about Lazarus's body, acknowledged the will of God; when He acknowledged the will of God, the Father was able to carry out His will for Lazarus.

Jesus Himself said in John 5:30: "I can of mine own self do nothing: as I hear, I judge: and my judgment is just; because I seek not mine own will, but the will of the Father which hath sent me." Jesus says, "As I hear, I judge." He was telling us that He couldn't do anything until He listened to the Father, and when He found the Father's will about a given situation, He was able to make the right decision. His decision was right because He sought not His will but the will of the Father that sent Him. "For I came down from heaven, not to do mine own will, but the will of him that sent me" (John 6:38).

Too much of our praying in order to know the will of God consists of asking and begging for something that may not be the will of God. Therefore, we waste a lot of time and a lot of energy begging, pleading, asking, wanting, and desiring that which God the Father is not about to give. More time needs to be spent in conforming our lives to the image of the Lord Jesus Christ rather than trying to beg God to do something that is not within His will. Then we would know that some things are not within His will. If we were more conformed to the image of the Lord Jesus Christ, then we would automatically know the will of God. Becoming Christlike is the easiest method in knowing the will of God, but it is the most difficult. This method is easy because the Lord Jesus will live out His life in us if we will let Him. This method is difficult because we don't want to yield our stubborn wills to Him, for yielding to God involves knocking self off the throne of our lives and enthroning the Lord Jesus.

God is endeavoring to bring us into the likeness of His Son (Rom. 8:29). If we could ever understand that God is trying to make us like Jesus, if we could ever come to exemplify the life of the Lord Jesus Christ by our thoughts, actions, and words, then we could know the will of God on a day-by-day basis.

If I am to know the will of God, and if I am to determine the will of God, I must be willing to live my life like the life of the Lord Jesus Christ. In other words, the more I live like Jesus, the more I will know the will of God for my life, and the more I conform to the image of the Lord Jesus Christ, the more I am able to know what the Father is already doing. The will of God is that which the Father is doing in heaven. Once we learn to check in with the Father to find out what He's doing, and then do it on a daily basis, we will be able to do what He wills for us.

Become Properly Related
to the Lord Jesus

If we are to know the will of God by living our lives like the life of the Lord Jesus Christ, we must become rightly related to the Lord Jesus Christ. This thought assumes first of all that we have been saved. We cannot know the will of God outside of being saved. The first will of the Father is for us to be saved. And until we are saved by "repentance toward God, and faith toward our Lord Jesus Christ," we can never know the will of God (Acts 20:21). But once we have been saved, there are some other things that must be done in our lives.

Confession of our sins to the living Lord is a must. We confess to the Father our wrongs, our mistakes, and anything the Bible calls sin that we have committed. Also, we have to be willing to confess that our ability is really nothing. Even Jesus said that He could do nothing but what he saw the Father do (John 5:19). Jesus chose to do only what He heard the Father saying and what He saw the Father doing. And once He chose to do what the Father was saying and was doing, He could fit into the perfect will of God. Jesus said, "Without me ye can do nothing" (John 15:5). Jesus had already said without the Father He "could nothing," and now He says, "Without me ye can do nothing."

Next we commit our lives to the Lord Jesus Christ. Someone asked, "Does that mean 99 percent?" Jesus Christ always committed Himself to the will of the Father 100 percent of the time. And because He made such a commitment of His life, He always was able to know what the will of the Father was. If we would make such a commitment, we could know His will. And certainly if we know His will, we will do it. When Jesus walked into the garden of Gethsemane, He talked to the Father about His approaching death. Jesus could see Himself dying for sinners, but He also saw Himself dying at the hands of sinners. Our Lord was asking the Father, "Is there not some other death that I can experience rather than death at the hands of sinners, the very ones for whom I am dying?"[1] Without waiting for an answer, Jesus said, "Father, if thou be willing, remove this cup from me: nevertheless not my will, but thine, be done" (Luke 22:42). (See Chapter 11.)

How may we know we are rightly related to the Lord Jesus Christ? The Lord Jesus Christ says we may know we are saved when we have joy that's overflowing, when our prayers are answered, and when we are able to be the witnesses that God wants us to be.

Get into God's Presence

The psalmist said, "Thy way, O God, is in the sanctuary" (77:13). The sanctuary refers to the presence of God. Thus, God's way can be found in His presence. Notice that the psalmist also discovered the tragic end of the wicked when he went into the sanctuary of God (Ps. 73:17). If we can find the way of God, if we can find the will of God, if we can find the purposes of God, if we can find what God wants us to do in His presence, then we should want to get into the presence of God. The psalmist had a great need in his life; he was discouraged and despondent. He didn't understand why so many wicked people were getting rich, and he had nothing; finally, he said, "I had an extreme migraine headache" (73:16, Author).[1] Therefore, he went into the sanctuary of God—into the presence of God. And when he went into the presence of God, he waited on God. While he waited on God, he worshiped God. Then when he worshiped God, he received the answer. God's way was so plain that the psalmist referred to himself as a "beast" before God for failing to see it (73:22).

We too can look around us and become discouraged and defeated. We can listen to what the world has to say through all news media possible, and we will be discouraged. We can hear people predict doom for the future and become discouraged. The psalmist said that the way of God can be found in the presence of God, and God's presence is anywhere that God is: in the house of God, in a home dedicated to God, in a place of business, and in a factory where one is standing before a machine. Wherever God is, there is His will. When we find ourselves in God's presence, we should be able to know automatically what God is wanting to do in our lives.

When Moses got into the presence of God, he knew God's ways immediately. Moses was standing on the bank of the Red Sea; the Egyptian army was behind him, and Moses began to cry out unto God. When he turned around to look, Moses found himself in the presence of Almighty God. When we find ourselves in the presence of God, we will know the will of God or the way of God for our lives as Moses did.

> And it shall be when thy son asketh thee in time to come, saying, What is this? that thou shalt say unto him, By strength of hand the Lord brought us out from Egypt, from the house of bondage: And it came to pass, when Pharaoh would hardly let us go, that the Lord slew all the firstborn in the land of Egypt, both the firstborn of man, and the firstborn of beast: therefore I sacrifice to the Lord all that openeth the matrix, being males; but all the firstborn of my children I redeem. And it shall be for a token upon thine hand, and for frontlets between thine eyes: for by strength of hand the Lord brought us forth out of Egypt. And it came to pass, when Pharaoh had let the people go, that God led them not through the way of the land of the Philistines, although that was near; for God said, Lest peradventure the people repent when they see war, and they return to Egypt: But God led the people about through the way of the wilderness of the Red Sea: and the children of Israel went up harnessed out of the land of Egypt (Ex. 13:14-18).

Some things that God says to us may seemingly be impossible, or they could be abnormally demanding. When Moses obeyed God's commands, God did exactly what He said He would do, and the children of Israel marched out on the other side, dry and safe.

The Bible says that we can come into the presence of

God.[2] First, we must realize that God's presence is available. God has taken the initiative. Christ Jesus died on the cross. When He died, the veil in the temple was torn, and He gave us the right to approach God. We can walk boldly into the holy of holies and talk to God for ourselves (Heb. 4:16). Whatever the circumstances, without the help of anyone else, we can go directly to God and find His way.

Second, we must recognize that God is the only answer. Too many people run around trying to find an answer from everybody else when God has said that He wants us to come to Him, having confessed our sins up to date, having committed our lives to the Lord, and having rightly related ourselves to Him through the Lord Jesus Christ. God wants us to enter into His presence. He is the source. He has the answers.

Third, we must repent of any self-claimed ability. A person whose life operates out of His own mind and will becomes a victim of pride, and repentance has to take place. No one can live the Christian life without Christ. God has never said that we could, but He has said that He would live the Christian life through us. Therefore, we need to change our minds about ourselves and start trusting God for His presence.

Fourth, we must respond to the light that comes. If we have obeyed these commands, then we should have light from God's Spirit. And when we have light in our hearts from the Holy Spirit and enlightenment from the Word of God, we can act upon the light. We can make our decisions, we can follow His way, and we can obey His will. And we can know that we are in the presence of God when we know the way of God for our lives.

Abide in His Presence[3]

Some people determine the will of God by flipping a coin. Most likely they are right 50 percent of the time, but that means they are also wrong 50 percent of the time. Two high-school sweethearts who had been married to others several years found each other at a class reunion. Both decided to drop their companions and start living with each other. They followed through on their decision because they believed that God had reunited them. Wrong, wrong, wrong! God had nothing to do with such an illicit affair.

Jesus said that we are to abide in Him as He abides in us. That means that we are to continually abide in Him as He continuously abides in us. The Bible does not say abide with Him; it says abide in Him. This statement does not mean that we are to live with Him but that we are to live in Him. The Bible does not say that we are to walk with Him but that we are to walk in Him.

In the Old Testament, the people of God walked with God. Enoch walked with God (Gen. 5:22,24). But in the New Testament one is to "walk in the Spirit" (Gal. 5:16). If we are to know the will of God, we must continuously abide in Him. The Lord Jesus Christ is our environment. We are to live in His environment. We are to be surrounded by Him. Everything we are is to be watched over by Him. We are to be centered in the Lord Jesus Christ. When we live in Him, we live from Him. He is our breath, our blood, and our all.

The Lord Jesus Christ is the Vine, and we are the branches. The Vine is constantly flowing out into the branches. And if we become cut off from the Lord Jesus Christ, the Vine, then we become fruitless and helpless.

But as we stay connected to Jesus as the branch is to the vine, then He flows through us. Thus, we can do all things through Christ who strengthens us (Phil 4:13). Even Jesus said that we could do greater works, have our prayers answered, and know the will of God when we are abiding in Him.

The will of God is something to which we submit. If Jesus Christ is abiding in us, and we are submitting to him, and He is supplying our every need, then we are in the will of God, and we can know the will of God, and we can do the will of God. Once we submit to God's will, then that will becomes the power to do anything and everything that God wants us to do. When we are willing to let God fill our lives, then God gives us power to live and do whatever He wills for us to do. In our prayers we do not have to move God, because whatever we ask that is according to His will, God has already willed, prepared, and stored. God actually waits for us to move earth in line with heaven so He can supply our every need and give us what He wanted to give us in the first place.

Through prayer we partake of God's graciousness. God's supply is already prepared. It's just a matter of our getting into the right position and living the right kind of life and abiding in His presence so we can have the supply for every need in our lives. We have the needs already met in our lives by the supply of the Lord. If our fellowship with God is right, we can become of one mind with Him about His will.

Billy Graham said that the will of God will never take us where the grace of God cannot sustain us. That kind of grace must be abundant and overflowing. If we are constantly in communion with the Lord Jesus Christ, who abides in us, then we are constantly knowing the will of

God. Therefore, we can constantly do the will of God in our lives.

Living like the Lord Jesus Christ involves constantly claiming the presence of God and the blessings of God in our lives. The branch, as long as it is connected to the Vine, can constantly claim the life of the Vine. And the Vine's life flows from the Vine into the branches. So can we as Christians, being the branches, have Christ Jesus, the Vine, flowing in and through us, enabling us to claim the presence of God and the blessings of God at all times. For we the believers have a guarantee that our attachment to Christ is eternal. All that Jesus is and all that He has belongs to us.

The Bible says we have not because we ask not (Jas. 4:2). So many of us today are not receiving because we are not asking, and many of us who are asking are not receiving because we are not abiding in Christ. We can live a quality of life which allows us to ask for anything, and it will be given to us. That life is available to us, and that quality of life will change our desires. The problem: we don't want to abide in Christ and have Christ abide in us. We are to live our lives where our wills and His will merge. Moreover, this life of abiding is a life of asking what we will, and it will be done unto us.

Jesus lived such a quality of life that He could ask what He desired, and that desire was always fulfilled. Jesus said that he would give us the same kind of life with the same kind of results. Thus, if we abide in Jesus, we can get anything we ask for. But remember, it is our wills harmonizing with His will that makes the difference. And we may know that we are abiding in Christ when we are getting what we want.

The psalmist said, "Delight thyself also in the Lord; and

he shall give thee the desires of thine heart" (Ps. 37:4). Most of us have majored upon the word *desires*. The emphasis should be on the word *delight*. If delighting in God became the priority in our lives, it would not be long until our wills would be coinciding with His will. And when our wills harmonize with His will, and God's will harmonizes with ours, we will get what we want. But we may not be getting all we want right now because we've been majoring upon our desires, and God says that we are to major upon delighting in Him. This concept means that we are to be surrounded and enveloped by the Lord Jesus so He is everything to us. He is our all. He is everything we want. Wanting only Jesus will eliminate about 90 percent of our other wants. Then when we find that we only want Jesus, the other 10 percent of our wants will be brought into our lives. (See chapter 11.)

Phillip Brooks, one of the great preachers of the past, was a dynamic pulpiteer. People looked at him, watched him, and listened to him. One day while he was walking across a college campus, a person saw him and said, "Look, there goes Jesus." They could say that because he read so much about Jesus, thought about Jesus, talked about Jesus, and just lived like Jesus that he became the Jesus man as he walked on the campus. And living like Jesus is what God wants. Becoming like Jesus will enable us to know and to do the will of God for our lives. Manley Beasley is also the embodiment of these principles. He, too, is able to know the will of God because he abides in the Lord's presence.

5

Doing the Will of God

A few years ago, I did not follow the principles as set forth in this book in the purchase of a new car and a new maroon suit. I bought both on impulse. And the Lord allowed me to keep both longer than the normal. It seemed neither would wear out. After the church gave me a new car, I allowed my son to take the older car, and I finally moved the suit to one side of my closet. Everytime I wore the suit, it seemed to turn redder as a reminder that I had bought it on impulse. But praise the Lord, He is forgiving.

If there is a need in our lives, it is not so much to discover the will of God but to do it. Jesus said that we could discover God's will by doing it (John 7:17). "If any man will do his will, he shall know of the doctrine, whether it be of God, or whether I speak of myself." This Scripture gives a plain and simple truth. If we are to know the will of God, we must do it. Now Jesus is not contradicting these various biblical methods of discovering the will of God. He is saying that too often we spend too much time in seeking the will of God rather than in doing it. Also, He is saying that we spend too much time in seeking the will of God for our total lives when God is interested in giving only a partial plan for our lives or even a day-today plan. Only those who desire to do the will of God will realize that the word is from God. Jesus is not talking about the mechanical performance of God's will, for that is not enough. There must be an inclination toward Christ Jesus to make our conduct agree with His will.

If we will get out of our comfortable homes, churches, and places of work and start doing what we already know God desires for us to do—loving our enemies, going the second mile, giving our overcoats, turning the other cheek, forgiving 490 times for the same offense, witnessing and sharing Christ, and so forth—then God will reveal His will to us as it is needed in our lives.[1] George Mueller said: "Nine tenths of the difficulty is overcome when our hearts are ready to do the Lord's will, whatever it may be. The difficulty arises when we ask God to reveal His will before we are ready to do it unreservedly."

Paul said, "Wherefore be ye not unwise, but understanding what the will of the Lord is" (Eph. 5:17). Then he added that doing the will of God requires being filled with the Spirit, mutually submitting to each other as companions, loving one another, obeying parents, treating children, employers, or employees right.

The psalmist said, "Thy word is a lamp unto my feet, and a light unto my path" (119:105). We do not need to know the whole plan for our lives because God has promised to provide just the light needed for the next step or the next few feet along the path. It is difficult for us to appreciate this Scripture with modern technology being able to provide light for miles rather than for a few feet. The little lamp made by the people of the psalmist's day could be fitted onto the people's feet or possibly onto their sandals. But we don't want to move that slowly. We are in a hurry. Being in a hurry is different from what the

Bible says. "Wait on the Lord: . . . wait, I say, on the Lord" (Ps. 27:14). But there is a reward for waiting on the Lord. "But they that wait upon the Lord shall renew their strength; they shall mount up with wings as eagles; they shall run, and not be weary; and they shall walk, and not faint" (Isa. 40:31). What a promise!

Assume that We Are
in the Will of God

So often we are made to feel that we must not be in the will of God. An offer comes to move up the ladder of success whether in the secular or sacred world. We assume that we are not where we ought to be, else the offer would not have come. So we begin to search for God's will in the matter. An offer to move is not necessarily the will of God for us. The offer may be only an opportunity to pray. God does enjoy fellowship with His children. He made us to bring pleasure to Him (Rev. 4:11). In fact, He has chosen us (2 Tim. 2:4) and commanded us (Heb. 4:11) to bring pleasure to Him. He wants us to bring pleasure to Him.

If we assume an offer is not necessarily the will of God, then we must assume that we are in the will of God where we are. Of course, we could never consider ourselves to be in the will of God if we are involved in sinful practices or sinful occupations. Sin short-circuits our prayer life and places us outside of God's will.

Here is where we wait on the Lord. Moving at the first opportunity may mean jumping from the frying pan into the fire. Many young adults find themselves moving from one job to another, thinking that the next job will be the right one. Regardless of the work, the pay, or the benefits, the job may not be the right one. But God does have a

right one. Christian business persons sometimes fail because they align themselves with an unsaved partner.
This type of partnership is a violation of a scriptural command: "Be ye not unequally yoked together with un-
believers" (2 Cor. 6:14). Often some business partners
want to follow unscrupulous business practices to make a
quick dollar. But the Christian has a conscience to deal
with as well as guilt feelings when one is involved in
wrong. The risk is too great. The best scriptural advice is
to wait on the Lord, for waiting on the Lord can be God's
will for the here and now.

If suddenly more people would assume that they are in
the will of the Lord where they are, there would be greater peace, fewer ulcers, less pill taking, less complaining,
and less wasted energy. Let us take time right now to
thank the Lord for our jobs, our situations. To do so would
place us in the will of God. "In every thing give thanks:
for this is the will of God in Christ Jesus concerning you"
(1 Thess. 5:18). It is the will of God to be satisfied where
we are. The apostle Paul knew how to be content in every
situation, good or bad (Phil. 4:11-12). (See chapter 11.)

It is the will of God to accept and use our spiritual gifts
(Rom. 12:6-8). It is human nature to be dissatisfied with
what God has given and to look at what God has given to
somebody else and wish we had their gifts. We are commanded to put our gifts to work where we are. God never
gives a bad gift. He gives the best, and we should use that
gift for the glory of Christ.

Know that God Does Not
Have Two Wills for Us

One of the greatest things to learn in the doing of the
will of God is that God does not have two wills regarding

the same thing. This truth came to me very clearly a few years ago. Another church pulpit committee was definitely interested in my going before their church in view of a call to become their pastor. I had visited with the committee members on their church field. Everything looked fine. The committee felt good about me. They believed that it was the will of God for me to become their pastor. In my heart I had reached the place that I felt that I could be at peace in serving the Lord either in their church or in my present church. But I knew that serving in both churches was not possible. God could not want me in two places. So I called Brother Jack Taylor and told him of my dilemma. I asked him, "How could it be the will of God to be in either place?" Then Brother Jack gave me some practical wisdom by asking me some questions. Our Lord asked questions, too. Jack asked, "Were you in the will of God before you heard of the other church?" My reply was yes. Then he said, "You are still in the will of God now." And I agreed. Then Jack said, "If God wants you to move, He will need to give you a directive to go."

God does not have two wills for a given situation. He is not as pleased with our being in one place as another. He has a single will for us regarding any given situation. God can no more have two wills on a given concern for us than He can have two wills for the unsaved or the carnal. His will for the unsaved is their salvation (2 Pet. 3:9). But the unsaved have a choice—to obey that will or to reject that will. His will for the carnal is their sanctification (1 Thess. 4:3). And they, too, have a choice. But for both, a wrong choice leads to judgment later or now.

Expect God to Give Directions
When Change Is Needed

Jack Taylor's advice that I would need a directive from the Lord to move from Leawood to go to another place to serve Him settled my dilemma. Now I could wait on the Lord to give a directive. To me a directive did not mean an offer by the pulpit committee, a raise in salary, a second or third effort on the part of the committee; it meant that God must give me a directive in the form of a divine utterance. To others a directive might require some other avenue or expression. I wanted the Lord Jesus Christ to speak to my heart. The directive did not have to be audible, but God had to speak. I was in His will in my present situation, and I wanted to be in His will in my future service. So I prayed, waited, prayed, and kept on doing the will of God in my life. It was not a time of stopping or coasting but a time of doing His will in the place assigned to me by Him many years before. The directive did not come. Peace came to my heart. The anointing of God continued to be on the church and on my ministry. Ron Dunn said it well: "Faith is not idle; it works while it waits."[2]

The Lord may have us in a difficult situation, but the difficulty of the situation does not make it any less the will of God. Joseph was in a difficult situation many times after his brothers sold him into slavery. But when Joseph saw the totality of his ministry, he knew that he had been doing the will of God (Gen. 50:20).

When we make the wrong decision and run ahead of God, we will miss God's best for our lives. Complaining, whining, being scared, and wanting to die, Elijah found himself under a juniper tree. He had been running for his life, he thought. But the God Elijah served had given him his greatest victory at Mount Carmel just a few days before he ran. God was still gracious. Not once did God become upset with Elijah, but He continued to reach out to Elijah.

A pastor left a strong witnessing church and went to a dry, dead church. He knew that he had missed the will of God. But God was gracious. Because the pastor repented and prayed, and his friends prayed, he was given a new opportunity. This time the pastor obeyed and found the peace that he had sought.

Obey When God Gives a Directive

Continuing to do the will of God becomes automatic when a directive comes. Obedience is expected. It is assumed that we will obey when the directive is given. In fact, it is doubtful that a divine directive will come to one who is out of the will of God, unwilling to obey. God is not interested in revealing His will to us if we only want to consider it, enjoy it, brag about it, and refuse it. God gets into business with those who get into business with Him.

When Paul missed the will of God, he was not trying to find a way to disobey God and have his own way. The Holy Spirit, knowing the heart of Paul, blocked Paul's attempts to go into one country and issued a call to go into another. We do not have to know why. We just have to obey. That's what Paul did. When the Macedonian call came, he obeyed (Acts 16:10). "Immediately we endeavoured to go . . . assuredly gathering that the Lord had called us for to preach the gospel unto them," said Luke. All of us must be as willing and as prompt in obeying our directives and callings.

Many modern-day missionaries fit into this kind of calling and obeying. Doing the will of God in a church, hearing a call to change directions, and obeying that call, they continue to do the will of God on a mission field.

6

Receiving God's Truth

One of the members of the church walked up to me one day in the foyer and said, "I've been enjoying coming to church, hearing the Word, and getting it in my heart and life." That kind of statement will lift a preacher's heart. In fact, it'll almost send him into a spiritual orbit. Then the woman said, "There was a time that I didn't get anything out of the services and messages." It was time for me to say, "Oh, me." But she continued. "It was all my fault. I didn't come to get anything. I didn't come prepared. I was not ready to obey." Then she added, "I receive much more now that I know how to obey the Word."

If we are to know how to determine the will of God for our lives, we must know how to get truth from the head to the heart. Many people know Bible facts, but they know very little spiritual truth. It is a delight to hear people expound the Word. They know the facts, but they are able to give biblical truths, too, because they have been willing to obey them.

Natural persons cannot understand the teachings of the Lord Jesus Christ nor the truth of the Word because they have no spiritual knowledge and no spiritual discernment. Truth has never been dropped from their heads to their hearts. Paul said, "The natural man receiveth not the things of the Spirit of God: for they are foolishness unto him: neither can he know them, because they are spiritually discerned" (1 Cor. 2:14).

Even the saved, if they are carnal, have difficulty receiving truth. If one reads the Bible and never gets anything out of it, then something is wrong spiritually because God is ready to give truth. If carnality is in the life of the believer, that carnality has to go if that believer is to receive the truth.

The unspiritual person does not receive the truth. She knows facts. She can sometimes quote more Scripture or give more answers to more tricky questions from the Bible than the spiritual, but she does not know the truth. She has facts, and those facts are still lodged in her mind. She can take, use and debate those facts, but she often does not have truth that will guide her in her daily walk with Christ.

The unspiritual person is easily discerned. He's the one who teaches himself, who pushes his own ideas, who presses his own claims for position, power, and praise, and blows his own horn. There is a modern-day proverb which says, "He that tooteth his own horn, the same shall be heard. He that tooteth not his own horn, the same shall not be heard." But you know, there's a sequel to that. It says, "He that tooteth his own horn, the same shall run his own battery down." This kind of person will not receive revealed truth from the Holy Spirit because He'll not give it to the unspiritual.

God's desire is to drop truth from the head to the heart. This ministry of bringing truth to the heart is the work of the Holy Spirit. The Holy Spirit is the Spirit of truth. And this Holy Spirit, who is the Spirit of truth, magnifies Jesus and guides us into all truth (John 16:13). What a teacher everyone of us has indwelling us! Yet people say, "I don't know; I just can't get anything out of the Word." Such a statement means that they have not shared this fact with the Holy Spirit and asked Him to start controlling their lives and giving them truth from the Word of God. The Holy Spirit will bring truth to our hearts if we will just let Him do it, but we have to be willing to allow Him to bring us truth.

Paul articulated exactly how the Holy Spirit will drop truth from our heads to our hearts. The principles are set forth in Romans 10:14-21.

A Message to Believe

Truth will drop from the head to the heart when we have a message to believe. The Bible is our message to believe.

God has given us the written Word (*logos*). In Romans 10:15, Paul spoke of the written Word that can be our spoken Word: "the gospel of peace" or "glad tidings of good things!" "The *logos* is the message of the Lord, delivered with His authority and made effective by His power."[1] Thus, all of Romans 10 becomes a message about Christ.

The message is not only the gospel that we proclaim, but it is the Bible that we believe. The message is believable because it came from God. Thus, we need to study the Bible to learn its message. In other words, we will have to take time to read the Word. Half a minute here and a half a minute there are insufficient times with the Word. We must spend enough time with the Word if we are to have a biblical base through which God can speak.

Throughout the Bible the Lord commands us to read, study, meditate, muse, memorize, and hide the Word of

God in our hearts. Such activity with the Word is a time of fellowship with the sovereign God. Reading the Bible is more than keeping a discipline, enjoying a habit; it is praising and blessing the Lord as He communes with our hearts through the Word. (Restudy chapter 2.)

An Utterance to Hear

Truth drops from the head to the heart when there is an utterance of Christ to hear. In Romans 10:17, Paul said, "So then faith cometh by hearing, and hearing by the word of God." The Greek word for *word* is *rhema.*

Ron Dunn beautifully expresses the difference between *logos* and *rhema:*

> *Logos* is the Word; *rhema* is a word from the Word. *Logos* is the message; *rhema* is the message spoken; *Logos* is the content of the message; *rhema* is the communication of that message. In *logos* the emphasis is on substance; in *rhema* the emphasis is on sound. *Logos* is the entire Bible; *rhema* is a verse from the Bible.[2]

Thus the Word read or preached is taken by the Holy Spirit and made the utterance of Christ to our hearts. Christ speaks truth to our hearts. He makes the Word alive. He quickens our spirit and enables us to know and to believe His truth. Through the *rhema* God reveals to us His will for our lives. "All this means that there must be a spiritual hearing as well as a physical hearing, a quickening of our spirit by His Spirit that enables us to perceive the voice of Christ speaking to us through His Word."[3]

This concept that Christ speaks to our hearts conforms to Paul's words, "How shall they believe in him of whom they have not heard?" (Rom. 10:14). This part of the verse may be translated, "How shall they believe in him whom they have not heard?" (ASV) It is not "of whom" but "whom." The unsaved are able to believe as they have a direct and divine utterance of Christ to their hearts. So it is with the believer. He receives a divine utterance from Christ to his heart so he may have truth and through the affirmation of that truth to his heart may know God's will for a situation in his life.

When Christ speaks to our hearts, we shall be able to hear. He will enable us to hear His utterances. Thus, we shall know His will, but there are conditions to hearing His divine utterances.

Israel, we are told, heard but did not hear. The Israelites heard the message (*logos*), but they heard no divine utterance (*rhema*) because they were a "disobedient and gainsaying people" (Rom. 10:21). These Israelites had determined not to believe and obey God. Disobedience had become their life-style.

A review of the Bible will reveal many disobedient people. God's people often did not want to obey. Moses struck a rock when he was to speak to it. Saul was to destroy all of the camp of the Amalekites, but he kept back a part of the spoils (1 Sam. 15:9). When confronted by the prophet Samuel with the fact that he had disobeyed God, Saul weakly tried to cover his sin by saying he had saved the animals for a sacrifice to God (1 Sam. 15:15). Samuel stated the desire of God when he said, "Hath the Lord as great delight in burnt offerings and sacrifices, as in obeying the voice of the Lord? Behold, to obey is better than sacrifice, and to hearken than the fat of rams" (1 Sam. 15:22).

If being disobedient and argumentive prevented Israel from hearing God, then such sins will keep us from hearing Christ's utterances, too. And if we do not hear Christ in our hearts, then truth will not drop from our heads to our hearts. Turning the two negative attitudes of Israel into positive attitudes will reveal the two other conditions of getting truth to drop from the head to the heart.[4] These conditions also are enclosed in God's message from Samuel to Saul—to obey and to hearken.

A Resolve to Obey

Prior to reading the Word or to hearing the Word proclaimed, we must resolve by an act of our wills and in our spirits that we will obey whatever truth the Holy Spirit drops from our heads to our hearts. Truth first comes in the form of facts from the Bible or from the message being proclaimed from the Bible. Being willing to obey does not mean that we have to obey everything the Bible, preacher, or teacher says, but it does mean that we have to obey the truth that the Holy Spirit makes real by a divine revelation to our hearts.

Too often, people go to the Bible to read in their quiet time or to their place of worship as a part of a jury. They listen to all the facts and then make a decision. If these people go to church to hear all the facts from the one proclaiming the message before deciding what to do with them, they will not have truth to drop from their heads to their hearts nor know the will of God. One who is going to receive truth is one who is committed to obeying the truth when it comes. As followers of Christ Jesus, we must be willing to obey truth when it comes. And truth will drop to the heart. When God takes truth and drops it from the mind to the heart, this dropping is an experience; it is a revelation. We will not receive truth and thus know God's will unless we are willing to do what God desires of us.

Jesus is the classic example of knowing truth and knowing the will of the Father. Jesus was truth (John 14:6). He constantly obeyed the Father, and the Father constantly gave truth to Him. Within that truth, He discovered the directions for His life.

Committing ourselves to obeying prior to hearing truth in order to know the will of God may not seem to be rational or logical, but it is an expression of our faith in the living Lord and of our desire to know His will. And faith with commitment is what God honors. This kind of commitment is the same as taking a sheet of paper and signing our names at the bottom and then trusting God to fill in the blank space with His directions. God can be trusted. In fact, He *must* be trusted if we are to know His will.

A Determination to Hearken

Samuel gave the proper order, and his order is the same as found in Paul's letter to the Romans—to obey and then to hearken (Rom. 10:21). King Saul wanted to do what he himself desired. But Samuel gave to him what God desired most in a person's life: obeying and hearkening. In the Bible, people were often commanded to hearken unto the Lord (Deut. 27:9; 1 Kings 22:28; Ps. 34:11; 45:10; Prov. 7:24; Isa. 28:23; Mark 7:14; Acts 2:14; Acts 15:13; and Jas. 2:5).

Once we have settled the matter regarding obedience, then and only then are we ready to listen. God is not interested in dangling His will before us to see what we might do about His desire for us. He wants us to hearken unto Him.

Hearkening to the voice of God demands compliance or obedience at the end of the hearing. Unwillingness to obey God's commands causes us not to hear from God regarding His will. Thus, to be able to hear, we must be willing to hearken.

We are to hearken with expectancy. "It is God's responsibility to speak; ours to hear."[5] Therefore, we expect to hear a word from God that gives us directions for our lives, answers for problems, wisdom for our decisions, and supplies for our needs. We are to listen with excitement also. Excitement on hearing from God can become a part of expectancy. God wants to speak to us, and He wants us to be prepared to hear. Our expectancy will reach the height of excitement as we hear from God regarding His will.

An exciting moment came to me when I attended a revival service in another church. I was about ready to take some action concerning a serious matter. But that night I was open to truth from the Lord, and I was willing to obey whatever truth He dropped to my heart. During the service, the truth came. I became aware that I was about to run ahead of God and that God wanted me to wait on Him. During the invitation, the revivalist asked for people to stand and share what we were believing God to do. So I stood and shared that I was about to run ahead of God in a serious problem, but I was now trusting Him to take care of the situation because of the truth that God had given to me during the service. A few weeks later, God did take care of the problem in a way that was even startling to me. His solution was a cause of joy to all who were concerned about it.

7

Knowing Who's Speaking

Eli had difficulty in determining who was speaking to Samuel. Twice Samuel had heard the voice of God and had gone to ask Eli if he were calling (1 Sam. 3:1-18). Each time Eli missed the call of God to Samuel and told him to go back to bed.

Messages from the Lord were rare in the time of Eli. Because of carelessness, Eli had allowed his sons to profane their ministry among the people. Sin was in the camp. God had given a son to Hannah, who in turn had dedicated him to God and left him with the priest Eli. Little Samuel was growing physically and becoming popular. He had become the favorite of the people as well as the Lord's.

When Samuel came back the third time to Eli to inquire about Eli's needs, Eli recognized that Samuel was hearing the voice of God (v. 8). So Eli informed him to go back to bed, and when he heard the voice again to say, "Speak, Lord; for thy servant heareth" (v. 9). Then Samuel obeyed his master and went back to his place of rest.

Then the Lord came and called again to Samuel. This time Samuel was ready. He knew that the Lord was the one who was calling him. So he responded, "Speak, Lord;

for thy servant heareth." Then the Lord proceeded to give Samuel a message to deliver to Eli.

Eli was not alone when it came to understanding who was calling. Being a man of God in his nineties (1 Sam. 4:15), Eli should have recognized the voice of God, but he didn't. The Bible explains why Samuel did not understand at first. "Now Samuel did not yet know the Lord, neither was the Lord yet revealed unto him" (1 Sam. 3:7). What a contrast! Two people, one elderly who should have known the voice of God and one young who had not yet experienced hearing the voice of God to him, missed the call of God. But God was persistent. Eli, though slow, was able to detect what was happening. And Samuel was eager, trusting, and obedient. That combination will ultimately cause anyone to understand that it is God who is calling when the voice of God is being heard.

God speaks today. More often it is a still small voice rather than an audible one. Just the same, He speaks. Our problem is that we are afraid to say, "Speak, Lord; for thy servant heareth." Fear is the enemy to hearing the voice of God.

God wants us to know His will, and He wants to reveal it to us. Thus, He speaks to us. Listen to the Bible: "To-day if ye will hear his voice" (Heb. 3:7,15; 4:7). "My sheep hear my voice, and I know them, and they follow me" (John 10:27).

It is so easy to fall into a trap and want God to write out His instructions on a wall. If God were to write out instructions on a wall as He did to Belshazzar, our countenances would change, and our thoughts would trouble us as they did that king (Dan. 5:6). But God doesn't have to write on a wall, for God's putting His laws into our minds enables us to know His will, and His writing them in our hearts makes us want to obey them (Heb. 8:10). God wants us to do His will. And if God wants us to do His will, then He certainly is going to communicate it to us.

How may one know who is speaking? Only God truly knows what His will is, and thus He is the only one who can reveal it. But Satan is able to speak, as every believer knows. There are also the demands of self, and self can give some big impressions and whispers. Thus, the following suggestions may be used to determine who is speaking when a still small voice comes.

Satan

Satan will use anything or say anything to keep us from knowing or doing the will of God. Satan erects hindrances and obstacles so we will miss God's will. Satan is opposed to God and His will, and he wants no one to do it.

From the beginning, Satan entered his ugly head into the Garden of Eden to thwart the will of God. And through the centuries since, he has not left us. He caused Adam and Eve to sin, Cain to murder Abel, Noah to get drunk, Abraham to fear and claim his wife as his sister, the brothers of Joseph to sell him into slavery, the Israelites to rebel in the wilderness and even in the Promised Land, the favored people to sin and be sent into captivity, the religious leaders to reject Jesus Christ as Lord and Savior, and the churches to be less than what Jesus intended for them to be in Him.

Satan can counterfeit any God-given experience and any God-spoken word. He is a master at deception and the father of all lies. He is subtle and crafty. Thus, Satan is able to speak to people in many ways or to jam the communication lines of God.

Communists are masters in deception and lying, espionage, and counterespionage. They are able to jam the wavelengths of the broadcasts being beamed into their country so that its message is warbled and cannot be received. Those who do not speak the truth cannot endure the truth when it is presented. Jesus said that it is the truth that sets people free. Communists cannot be set free because freedom is a great threat to their ideology. Neither can the devil afford to allow the truth of Christ to get through to a person, for truth will set a person free and make that person want to do the will of God.

How may one know that it is Satan who is speaking instead of the Lord? Satan contradicts the Word of God. Whenever an impression or word makes its way into our mind that contradicts the Word of God, we may know that it is from Satan and not from God. Satan is afraid of the Word of God. James said, "Submit yourselves therefore to God. Resist the devil, and he will flee from you" (Jas. 4:7). We resist the devil with the Word of God.

Satan appeals to the flesh. He bypasses the inner nature called the spirit which is the dwelling place of the Holy Spirit. He appeals to the soulish part of a person through the bodily appetites.

> Let no man say when he is tempted, I am tempted of God: for God cannot be tempted with evil, neither tempteth he any man: But every man is tempted, when he is drawn away of his own lust, and enticed. Then when lust hath conceived, it bringeth forth sin: and sin, when it is finished, bringeth forth death (Jas. 1:13-15).

> Love not the world, neither the things that are in the world. If any man love the world, the love of the Father is not in him. For all that is in the world, the lust of the flesh, and the lust of the eyes, and the pride of life, is not

of the Father, but is of the world. And the world passeth away, and the lust thereof: but he that doeth the will of God abideth for ever (1 John 2:15-17).

Satan stymies the growth of the Kingdom. Satan's words will not create growth within the kingdom of God. He has no interest in people being saved or becoming Christlike in character. His desire is to retain all people for himself. He did not want Jesus to die on the cross, and he does not want people to accept the Christ of the cross.

Satan delays through procrastination. "Why do a thing today when you can do it tomorrow?" is Satan's motto. He never gets in a hurry unless it is to capture what he is about to lose.

He that committeth sin is of the devil; for the devil sinneth from the beginning. For this purpose the Son of God was manifested, that he might destroy the works of the devil (1 John 3:8).

Satan gives a false sense of security. He promises freedom, satisfaction, and self-realization. Yet there is no peace. He led the church of Laodicea to say, "I am rich, and increased with goods, and have need of nothing"; even though the people were "wretched, and miserable, and poor, and blind, and naked," and in need of counsel (Rev. 3:17).

Jesus answered them, verily, verily, I say unto you, Whosoever committeth sin is the servant of sin (John 8:34).

Be not deceived; God is not mocked: for whatsoever a man soweth, that shall he also reap. For he that soweth to his flesh shall of the flesh reap corruption; but he that soweth to the Spirit shall of the Spirit reap life everlasting (Gal. 6:7-8).

Satan accuses God of making people lose out on the good life. He caused the rich farmer to say, "Soul, thou hast much goods laid up for many years; take thine ease, eat, drink, and be merry" (Luke 12:19). It was also Satan who caused Eve to question God's warning about the wages of sin, God's withholding of something good from her and life's fulfilling qualities (Gen. 3:1-6). But Eve tried Satan's way and suffered immensely as a result. Satan has no good ways. The writer of Hebrews said that the pleasures of sin are for a season. Such pleasures are temporary at their best (Heb. 11:25).

Satan says trials are because of God's lack of love. He is so subtle. He says that if God really loved us then He would not allow us to suffer. The friends of Job felt this way about life's trials and sufferings. Hoping he would break and admit his sins, Job's friends sat and stared at him for seven days. To them, suffering was the result of sin. Whatever the cause of suffering, the devil accuses God of failing to love us. At first it sounds quite plausible. To the Israelites, this suggestion was within the realm of the possible. How could a God of love allow them to suffer?

If God allowed only blessings to come into our lives, then we'd forget Him (Hos. 13:6). Trials, large and small, come upon us. They may be "the tiny pin-prick troubles that annoy, the squeaking wheels that grate upon our joy."[1]

Thanking and praising the Lord, whether we feel like it or not, can liberate us from the constant accusations of Satan or the murmurs from within. (See 1 Thess. 5:18, Eph. 5:20; and Heb. 13:15.)

Recently the devil unloaded his demonic attacks on me. They came in the form of criticisms, suggestions, and lies.

At times I felt that I was finished, washed up, and needed to quit. The more I became discouraged and depressed, the more the suggestions came into my mind. I had to resist the demonic with the Word of God, take my stand, and claim my position in Christ. And when I did, Satan and his demons had to flee.

How did I know that it was Satan and not God talking to me? Satan brought up things that I had confessed to God. God never reminds us about the things that we have confessed to Him. Too, I experienced the victory when I took my stand. Christ was sufficient for my trials. He delivered because He is the Deliverer.

Self

Self, being the sin nature and the source of our sins, also speaks to us. And if we listen to the self nature, it will produce sins. The only way to have victory over our sins is to have victory over self. This is the reason Paul says that we should mortify or put self to death (Col. 3:5). God has only one way to deal with self, and that is through death. We are to reckon ourselves as dead. "Likewise reckon ye also yourselves to be dead indeed unto sin, but alive unto God through Jesus Christ our Lord" (Rom. 6:11).

We reckon ourselves as dead to sin by saying no to self. We meet every suggestion from self with a resounding no. We appropriate Christ's death as our death. We take up our cross daily (Luke 9:23). By an act of our wills, we accept our death, willingly accepting our place on the cross of Calvary. For it was there that we died. We can believe, accept, and appropriate His death constantly. Then we can count on the life of Christ in us as making us to be alive in Him. "I am crucified with Christ: nevertheless I live; yet not I, but Christ liveth in me: and the life which I now live in the flesh I live by the faith of the Son of God, who loved me, and gave himself for me" (Gal. 2:20).

Self is constantly talking to us. When a driver of a car in back of us at a red light blows his horn because we fail to start as quickly as the light turns green, self says, "Don't let him get away with that; just wait through another cycle of red and green lights."

Let us recall that moment when someone laughed at our mistake. Self said, "Blast him for it." Let us remember the time someone criticized us. Self said, "Tell her where she was wrong. Do it right now." If someone mentions our weight or our habit or our weakness, self becomes irritated very quickly, and we are ready to strike with a hot iron or with a fiery tongue.

Self causes us to talk, and, oh, how talk gets us into trouble! If we are sensitive to the Holy Spirit, we usually have to confess to the Lord and to the person to whom we spoke sharply or critically.

Self demands its rights, insists on its own plans, and wants its own way. "It is always self who gets irritable and envious and resentful and critical and worried. It is self who is hard and unyielding in its attitudes to others. It is self who is shy and self-conscious and reserved."[2]

Brokenness is the need. Jesus was broken for us. He willingly accepted the cross.

> Let this mind be in you, which was also in Christ Jesus: Who, being in the form of God, thought it not robbery to be equal with God: But made himself of no reputation, and took upon him the form of a servant, and was made in the likeness of men: And being found in fashion as a man, he humbled himself, and became obedient unto death, even the death of the cross (Phil. 2:5-8).

To be broken means that we must accept the fact that we have no rights before human beings or God. Brokenness is not a mere surrendering of our rights but a recognition that we do not deserve anything except hell. When we are nothing and have nothing, then we hear nothing from self. Self seeks its own glory and wants the praise of others. And if self cannot get the praises of others, it will praise itself.

Herod sought and received human praise. Upon completion of his speech to the people of Tyre and Sidon, the people "gave a shout, saying, It is the voice of a god, and not of a man. And immediately the angel of the Lord smote him, because he gave not God the glory: and he was eaten of worms, and gave up the ghost" (Acts 12:22-23). Herod was not the first, and he will not be the last, to seek such glory. But God is to be glorified in all we do (1 Cor. 6:20).

Self enjoys sudden impulses, and such a self is constantly being bombarded with impulses whenever crises occur. Sudden impulses are not divine impressions; rather they are basically the desires of the flesh. For this reason people who have a tendency to drink alcoholic beverages will turn to such drinking when a problem arises, or a church member will revert to worry when an impossible crisis arises. An impulse comes, and being oriented to impulse response, self then projects these impulses into the conscious part of self and acts accordingly.

Self ignores common sense. Self doesn't want what's best; it had rather assume or do the ridiculous. When a crisis arises, self says, "Exhaust yourself. Do without food. Get no sleep or rest. Prove your love by going and doing. Be a martyr." Common sense says, "Eat properly, take time for some rest and sleep. Trust in the Lord."

The psalmist said, "Fret not thyself." "Trust in the Lord, and do good;" "Commit thy way unto the Lord; trust also in him; and he shall bring it to pass." "Rest in the Lord, and wait patiently for him" (Ps. 37:1,3,5,7).

Self avoids guidance from others. Often the Lord seeks to guide us through the godly counsel of others as they will be affected by many of our decisions. What are their feelings as well as their desires about the decision? Have they given their impressions even though unsolicited? What is the counsel of praying friends? If they do not have a word to give, at least they can pray for us. Jesus says, "If two of you shall agree on earth as touching any thing that they shall ask, it shall be done for them of my Father which is in heaven" (Matt. 18:19). Instead of avoiding the counsel of others, one should "Hear counsel, and receive instruction, that thou mayest be wise in thy latter end" (Prov. 19:20).

Self often seeks a confirmation from the Bible for what it wants. A person must read the Bible devotionally, obediently, and understandingly if one is to find a word from the Word that gives directions for one's life. (See chapter 2.) One must read and study the Bible carefully if one is to determine what God wants. The Bible says for itself, "The entrance of thy words giveth light; it giveth understanding unto the simple" (Ps. 119:130).

"God's Word is not so much a floodlight showing us the whole path; it is more like a torch throwing light on the next few steps."[3]

Self covers up an unwillingness to acknowledge limitations. To acknowledge our weaknesses and limitations would make us less than complete in ourselves and would mean that we need assistance from another source. And that source to a believer is God. To turn to God means that we believe that God can give guidance to our lives. "In all thy ways acknowledge him, and he shall direct thy paths" (Prov. 3:6). Then our weaknesses, limitations, and handicaps become assets and assist us in our trust in His guidance. Running one's own life leads to sinful living or to independent living (Eph. 4:17-19) and is senseless and fatal. "But ye have not so learned Christ; . . . That ye put off concerning the former conversation the old man, . . . And be renewed in the spirit of your mind; And that ye put on the new man" (Eph. 4:20-24).

Self desires to be free from any obligation to God. Modern man doesn't want to be obligated to anything or anyone, not even to God. People can be turned away from God "through philosophy and vain deceit, after the tradition of men, after the rudiments of the world, and not after Christ" (Col. 2:8). Paul added to the ways that persons attempt to express their independence of God.

> For men shall be lovers of their own selves, covetous, boasters, proud, blasphemers, disobedient to parents, unthankful, unholy, Without natural affection, trucebreakers, false accusers, incontinent, fierce, despisers of those that are good, Traitors, heady, high minded, lovers of pleasures more than lovers of God; Having a form of godliness, but denying the power thereof: from such turn away (2 Tim. 3:2-5).

A person will never be what he ought to be until he quits listening to self, for self is not interested in doing the will of God nor even knowing the will of God. There is but one way for a person to be what he ought to be and that is: "Christ in you, the hope of glory" (Col. 1:27). Christ must be allowed to take over one's life completely and reign as Lord.

God

God speaks to His people. His voice can be heard in the heart and even in the head. Sometimes God speaks audibly. A person can know when God speaks. Just as Samuel heard God's voice and obeyed the instructions of Eli, we, too, can hear God's voice today. There are ways to know if God is the One speaking.[4]

God speaks in a gentle whisper. He usually does not shout. Exceptions may be noted, but to most of us, God uses the whisper to our hearts to reveal Himself and His way. When God got ready to speak to Elijah, He did not speak in the wind or in the earthquake but in a "still small voice" (1 Kings 19:12). Once when He did speak loudly to Israel, the people asked Moses to ask God not to do that again. God's voice was too awesome.

God speaks calmly. He does not get excited and start commanding. He shares what His directions are. He doesn't operate on crises or sudden impulses. He knows what He is doing. And God believes that a person must be willing to acquiesce if that person is to do the will of God. He didn't set His redemptive machinery up to operate haphazardly or spasmodically but smoothly and efficiently. God does not function only during the crises of life to get His will to be known. He is constantly revealing Himself through nature, the conscience, the Bible, and the Lord Jesus Christ.

God speaks definitely. He is never vague. You don't have to guess what He is saying. When He spoke to the prophets, they knew His message regarding their sins. When God spoke to the apostle Paul regarding the shipwreck off the island of Melita, Paul knew exactly what he had to do if all the passengers, guards, and sailors were to be spared (Acts 27:1-26).

God speaks simply. He is not complicated with his instructions; neither does he warble his tongue. When Israel sinned in the taking of Jericho and thus failed to take Ai, the instructions to Joshua were very simple. (Study Josh. 7:10-15). The Israelites had no trouble in carrying out the instructions and finding Achan, the guilty person.

God speaks to the ones who are ready to obey. Usually, God immediately wants our obedience when He speaks. To the unsaved God says, "To-day . . . harden not your hearts" (Heb. 4:7): "Behold, now is the day of salvation" (2 Cor. 6:2). There is to be no delay. Most of the commands in the New Testament are in the present tense. God does not primarily deal in the future; rather He deals in the here and now. He wants action now. Many of the commands are in the present tense. This tense is not a command for the future. It is a command for right now. Whatever God's guidance is for you, it is something to be obeyed immediately.

God points in one direction when He speaks. He does not have two wills for His followers. He is constantly revealing that will to us. He wants us to know which fork in the road or the direction to take at life's intersection. When there is the need to know, He will be there speaking. Paul had already received instructions to go to Rome. But when the ship on which he was riding to Rome was about to go aground and become wrecked in the treacherous waters and reefs, God gave directions once again. It was Paul who said "that all things work together for good to them that love God, to them who are the called according to his purpose" (Rom. 8:28).

God leads through faith and not through fear. If God so

desired, He could get us ready to listen and obey Him quickly. He could suddenly make all doors where they could not be opened. He could send an earthquake and pin us down in our homes. God wants us to step out in what we know to be His will as found in His Word by faith. It is faith that moves us to action. God constantly surrounds us with His Word and will and gives us the faith to trust Him enough to obey what we hear. His word to us is: "Trust in the Lord with all thine heart; and lean not unto thine own understanding" (Prov. 3:5).

God usually uses natural rather than sensational processes to guide us. True, He uses the sensational on occasion. An evangelist[5] was preaching in a church revival where nothing much was happening. One day the evangelist said, "God needs to hit this church." Just as he spoke these words, a strong gust of wind hit the front door, blew the door off of its hinges, and floated the door down the center aisle to the altar. Now, that is sensational. But most of the time, God works in the audience to move the hearts of the people to action through the singing, praying, and preaching about Jesus. The Holy Spirit adds power to that name, and something happens. Jesus Himself usually used boats to cross the lakes and ate food prepared and cooked by the people. But on occasion He used His supernatural power to walk on water and to feed the five thousand hungry men plus women and children.

God gives freedom in prayer when He speaks. Prayer is encouraged in the Bible. Prayer is our way of speaking to God and making our requests known to Him. He gives us the right to pray until He answers. When He speaks, freedom to pray with thanksgiving comes to our hearts. "Be careful for nothing; but in every thing by prayer and supplication with thanksgiving let your requests be made known unto God" (Phil. 4:6).

God speaks by revealing our faults and the needs of others. It is so easy to see the faults of others. Satan enjoys pointing out such faults, for in this way he gives us pride. Satan likes for us to have pride, but "Pride goeth before . . . a fall" (Prov. 16:18). But God is interested in showing us our faults. If we believe that we've had a word from God because we now can see the faults of others, we didn't get our word from God. The message came from Satan or self. God wants to show us the needs of others so we can minister to them. "Brethern, if a man be overtaken in a fault, ye which are spiritual, restore such an one in the spirit of meekness; considering thyself, lest thou also be tempted" (Gal. 6:1).

> With our eyes on Jesus, the cause and completer of our faith who, in view of the joy that lay ahead for Him, submitted to the cross, thought nothing of the shame, and is seated at the right hand of the throne of God. Compare your experience with His, who was willing to stand so much hostility from sinners against Himself, so that you may not become weary and despondent (Heb. 12:2-3, Berkeley).[6]

One morning as I lay in bed, my mind was constantly reviewing the facts surrounding a particular situation that I was experiencing. Some people had disappointed me. I really didn't understand their action. Many prayers had been said about the situation. Then, suddenly, that morning as I was praying, God began to give me reasons the situation should not have arisen (Ps. 5:3). It was as though God had audibly spoken to me even though He had not. Peace came to my heart. Now I knew the reasons for the situation, but I had to keep silent. As I was having my quiet time, the Lord gave me a verse which confirmed that I could not share what He had said. God had spoken twice, and that was sufficient.

God wants to talk to His children. The problem with most of us is that we are too busy or too worried to hear God when He speaks. "Be still, and know that I am God" (Ps. 46:10).

Corrie ten Boom asked herself, "How do I know that God is speaking?" She replied, "Because I listen often." When we listen to God often enough, we'll know that He is the one speaking to us and that He is the One giving leadership in our lives.

8

Operating Under the
Holy Spirit's Leadership

Making right decisions is possible if we operate out of our inner spirits as occupied by the Holy Spirit. The Holy Spirit does occupy our inner spirits if we are saved. "Know ye not that ye are the temple of God, and that the Spirit of God dwelleth in you?" (1 Cor. 3:16). (Also see 1 Cor. 6:19.) God wants us to operate out of the spirit because He has given us the Bible to guide us in our decision-making processes. When we operate out of our inner spirits, we will be knowing and doing the will of God and thus be making right decisions. The Holy Spirit will see to that.

Most people do not operate out of the inner spirit. The unsaved cannot, and many of the saved will not. Both groups function bodily and soulishly.

According to 1 Thessalonians 5:23, every person is a trinity: spirit, soul, and body. "And the very God of peace sanctify you wholly; and I pray God your whole spirit and soul and body be preserved blameless unto the coming of our Lord Jesus Christ." The most important part from God's point of view is spirit. The next most important part is the soul, and the least important part is the body. We usually reverse the order. To most people the body is the most important, the soul is next, and the spirit has little or no importance. Indeed, most people are totally ignorant of the spirit as a vital part of a person. Yet the entire destiny of an individual is determined by what happens, or usually what does not happen, in his or her spirit.

The Body

The body is the outer shell, space suit, or envelope in which the non-material part of a person lives. In 2 Corinthians 5:1, the body is called "our earthly house of this tabernacle." The body is like a portable tent which we carry around with us wherever we go. The body is the means by which two things are true of us: (1) We are functional. We do everything by the use of our bodies. If we look, we use our bodies. If we think, hear, taste, touch, write, stand, walk, sit, travel, see, or smell, we use our bodies. (2) We are recognizable. We are identified by our bodies and our bodily appearance. Therefore, when people see me go down the street, they say, "There goes Jerry Glisson," instead of saying, "There goes the body of Jerry Glisson." I am recognized by means of my physical features. The body is also the means by which we are world conscious, or conscious of our environment and surroundings which register upon the senses of the body. And if our bodies are "right," we will be healthy.

The Soul

In the Greek "soul" is the word *psyche* from which we get our English words *psychology, psychiatry, psychotherapy, psychosomatic,* and many other terms. Our soul is our psychological life. The soul is made basically of a combination of mind, emotions, and will. Therefore, the soul is the means by which we think, feel, and choose. We live mentally, emotionally, and volitionally by means of our soul.

What is the soul? "It's not some little empty space between the heart and the lungs. It is the storehouse of our emotions and desires, the part of us that loves and hates and thinks and wills and grieves and decides. It is what distinguishes us from each other, the thing that makes you 'you.' "[1]

Jesus asked, "For what shall it profit a man, if he shall gain the whole world, and lose his own soul?" (Mark 8:36). He was not talking about final destination (heaven or hell); He was talking about the possibility of a person losing his present identity as a true human being and sinking into a subhuman, more-animal-than-man-type of life. And aren't multitudes of people doing exactly that today in their degradation and lostness? What kind of a bargain would a person be making if he gained the whole world, but in the process lost his basic identity as a true human being made in the image of God? Yet multitudes are doing exactly that. They are more like animals, acting out of the body and soul, than people in whom the human spirit and the Holy Spirit are most important.

Our souls are also the means by which we are world conscious, or conscious of our own identity and personality. Through the soul we have an intellectual knowledge of God; that is, we know about God. If we only know about God, we may have many right answers and many plausible arguments, but that is not enough. If our souls are "right," we will be happy. *Happy* is a totally human, psychological word which describes an experience that does not require a relationship with God and which is based on "hap," "happenstance," "happenings," or "perhaps."

The Spirit

The most important part of the individual is the spirit. The spirit of a person is the innermost part of the person. The spirit is the part with which a person does business or communicates with God. God determined to have all His dealings with a person and to fulfill all His purposes through a person by means of the inner spirit which was made after His own likeness. God shares Himself with a person in the spirit of that person. Why? "God is a Spirit: and they that worship [know, trust, love, adore, honor, obey, submit to] him must worship him in spirit and in truth [genuineness, reality]" (John 4:24).[2]

In Proverbs 20:27, the Bible says, "The spirit of man is the candle [lamp][3] of the Lord, searching all the inward parts of the belly." A candle that is unlighted is still a candle, but it is not fulfilling its primary purpose. The candle is not giving light. If the candle is lighted, it is still a candle, but it is now fulfilling the purpose for which it was created. So it is with the spirit of a person. Until a person is born again (John 3:3,7) by the Spirit of God, one's inner spirit is like that unlighted candle; it is dead and dark and is not fulfilling the purpose for which God created it. When a sinner is born again by the divine miracle of the new birth in one's inner spirit, it is like lighting a candle that was previously dark and dead. The human spirit is now fulfilling the great purpose for which God created it since that spirit is now containing Him. God in the Spirit literally lives in the people who have been born from above!

One's spirit is the means by which he is God conscious, not as a matter of theory or intellectual belief but by a relationship established by a new birth and by fellowship of daily communion with God in the cooperation of one's spirits and His Spirit.

Through the human spirit we have Spirit-revealed knowledge. If we know God, then we have a heart relationship, an acquaintance knowledge. "And this is life eternal, that they might know thee the only true God, and Jesus Christ, whom thou hast sent" (John 17:3).

The person who knows God and walks in His Spirit communicates to others on a God level. God Himself will speak through that person to the deepest level of the person to whom He speaks. And there is a flow of divine life (John 7:37-39) through that person who "lives in the Spirit" and "walks in the Spirit."

If our spirits are right with God through Jesus Christ, then we will be holy. The real issue is: How holy is my spirit? How holy is your spirit? Our holiness depends absolutely upon a miracle in the inner spirit known as the new birth and a regular relationship after the new birth with the Lord Jesus Christ in the presence and power of the Holy Spirit who now lives in our spirits.

"Many professing Christians . . . will be quite *willing* to admit that the soul [spirit][4] has senses, duplicated with those of the body; that it has eyes with which it may see God; ears by which it may hear the inner voice; the sense of touch, and even of smell, by which to distinguish between the wholesome and the corrupt, between the air of Paradise and the breath of the pit. But they have never learned to exercise them, to note and act upon their earliest suggestion (Heb. v. 14). This is the cause of infinite failure, and keeps such Christians in the stage of babyhood."[5] The Bible says, "O taste and see that the Lord is good" (Ps. 34:8). "Hear, and your soul shall live" (Isa. 55:3).

The Flesh

The flesh is everything that human beings receive by their first birth. Jesus said, "That which is born of the flesh is flesh" (John 3:6). Because of the fall humans were reduced to psychophysical beings. The human spirit died in the fall, and thus the only remaining resources were those of body and soul. If Adam and Eve had checked on their bodies and souls the next day after they awoke outside of the Garden of Eden, they would have found their bodies very much alive and their souls alive as well. For they could think, feel, and decide just as always. They had managed to keep their bodies and souls together right through their revolt against God. But what they didn't know was that they died instantly in the all-important area of their lives, the human spirit.

J. Stafford Wright[6] said, "The spirit was the original control center in man." God originally dwelt in the human spirit. But the moment Adam sinned, God, who is Spirit, moved out. Sadly, but respecting their free choice, God honored their decision to live independently of Him; and they died spiritually. In that moment, the human spirit became a death chamber; all of the lights went out in the inner spirit. Now, since that time, every person born of Adam (with one exception—Jesus) has been born with a dead spirit, or spiritually dead. The moment of Adam's fall is what is called "the fall of man" because humanity actually fell into a subhuman state. God must be in humanity for humans to be human.[7] Thus, human beings became something a great deal less than God intended for them to be. They became more animal than human. When a person says, "I'm not all here today," he is probably more truthful than he realizes. Most people are not all here; they are only two-thirds here, alive in body and soul but stone dead in spirit. And they do not know the difference for the simple reason no one can convince a dead person that he is dead.

In the fall, every person came out the loser. Every person would be born dead in his or her spirit. God would no longer dwell there. Every one would also be born with a spiritual "compartment" that is empty and with a tendency to sin. This tendency is of such nature that every person will choose to sin when he reaches the age where he understands that he has a choice either to do right or to do wrong. Something else happened in the fall of man even worse than the forfeiture of God's presence. Every person became egocentric. From the moment of the fall the *I* would predominate. And this principle of egocentricity is biblically called "the flesh." (This is not to be confused with the human body.) The flesh has its origin and roots in the devil himself (Rom. 7:18; Rom. 8:3). In the fall the human mind, emotion, and will fell under the influence and control of Satan; the body also became an instrument of unrighteousness (compare Rom. 6:16). "Thus man became infinitely worse than an animal, for emptied of his divine content, and his soul invaded by the flesh, the animal part of him became the plaything and the workshop of the devil himself."[8]

Thus, unredeemed man is not mere animal, for he still retains a human spirit, a capacity for God. This capacity for God makes it possible for him to become spiritually regenerative by faith in Christ Jesus.

The flesh continues as a factor opposed to God in a saved person. The flesh can never be put to death once and for all by us; dying to the flesh is to be a continuous activity. And if the flesh is not kept in control by submis-

sion to the Lord Jesus Christ, there will be no progress in
the Christian life nor the discovery of the will of God for
one's life.

The body is an initiator. It initiates action. It makes
demands. It calls for a response. The body has direct ac-
cess to the soul (mind). To register its needs, the body
sends its signals to the brain, the seat of the mind. The soul
(mind) is the responder; it is never the initiator. Being the
responder, the mind determines how it will satisfy the
body. For thirst, it may suggest water, a carbonated drink,
or even an alcoholic beverage.

The Bible speaks of the body/soul combination as the
fleshly part of humanity. People can live and make decisions without ever being aware of the inner spirit—which
is dead in the unsaved—or without listening to the other
initiator, the divine Spirit living in the inner spirit in the
nongrowing Christian.

The Holy Spirit living inside of a person's inner spirit is
not a responder. He is an initiator. He initiates action. He
calls for a response. (See John 16:8-11). Again the soul
(mind) is the responder to the Spirit's promptings. The
soul (mind) faces a choice, whether to listen to the body
or to the indwelling Spirit.

Even though we have been restored to life by the presence of the Holy Spirit, who is now prompting us from
within our human spirit, the flesh which was not eradicat-
ed at the time of the new birth is still operative within the
believer's life. And that flesh will lead to the wrong choice
unless the Spirit is allowed to be in control. So by an act
of our wills, we need to choose to put to death the flesh
and at the same time choose to allow the Lord Jesus to live
in and through us. And when the Lord Jesus is allowed to

live out His life in and through us, right choices can be made.

A change of mind and a change in attitude and outlook in the heart of the believer are needed. For it was Christ who died and rose again to introduce an entirely new principle of human behavior of living to and for Christ which is to "walk in the Spirit"! But if this new principle is not allowed to work in our lives, then the old principle of human behavior of living to and for ourselves, which is to "walk after the flesh," will dominate our decision-making processes. We will be dominated either by God or by Satan.

Operating Out of the Flesh

Persons who operate out of the flesh are their own bosses. They act independently of God. When a decision needs to be made, they have to depend upon their own abilities, education, training, mental powers, and others' thoughts and capabilities. Many times they will derive the right answers, arguments, decisions. But there is no Spirit within the inner spirit to give assistance to the decision-making process. They are their own, freewheeling, and following any impulse they choose whether the impulse be provoked by Madison Avenue techniques, super sales pitch, or any other stimulus from their surroundings. Humanism is their best source of help. They can do only what persons can do. And by a surface look at our technological world, that kind of person is doing fairly well according to natural standards, but he or she is failing, too. Such a person uses a trial-and-error method until success comes. The inward look often reveals frustration, confusion, failure in the home, and spiritual bankruptcy.

Many times these persons do not know the end result

of their decisions, especially if there is uncertainty in the decisions to be made. They have no higher power to consult. The natural life cannot do God's will, live as God requires, or do God's work. Often natural persons resort to alcoholic beverages to clear the mind, they say. But such drinks only dull the mind. Instead of making better decisions, they make worse ones. Natural or soul knowledge is all that they possess.

The natural person often scoffs at God. "They are corrupt, and speak wickedly concerning oppression: they speak loftily. They set their mouth against the heavens, and their tongue walketh through the earth" (Ps. 73:8-9). "The fool hath said in his heart, There is no God" (Ps. 53:1). (Compare Jude 16-19.) Yet, God says, "Pride goeth before destruction, and an haughty spirit before a fall" (Prov. 16:18).

Human reason, natural judgment, and common sense are good as far as they go, but they do not go nearly far enough. Madness is usually the verdict of the world's wisdom concerning God's work. Whenever a person allows the natural mind to take precedence, that person becomes bewildered and paralyzed and soon looks for help from another humanistic source.

Operating Out of the Spirit

Once we have invited the Holy Spirit into our lives by trusting the Lord Jesus Christ as our Savior and have yielded our lives to the control of the Spirit, then we can begin to function as God intended.

We have an Initiator living in us who is always right. He never makes a mistake. We may make mistakes, but He never makes one. How do we make ourselves available for His help? We yield ourselves to the Holy Spirit's control.

"Be filled with the Spirit" (Eph. 5:18), and "Walk in the Spirit" (Gal. 5:16). "If we live in the Spirit, let us also walk in the Spirit" (Gal. 5:25). Rather than listening to the demands of the body, we listen to the Holy Spirit within our spirit. We make decisions based upon His enlightenment.

The inner spirit is the organ of spiritual knowledge. Paul's prayer was that we might be "filled with the knowledge of his will in all wisdom and spiritual understanding (Col. 1:9). "Understanding implies a sense or apprehension of the fuller meaning of what is known, with the ability to apply that knowledge to adequate value. It is a matter of intuitive recognition or perception of the hidden nature and trend of things"[9] Spiritual understanding is more than natural intelligence. "It is that faculty of the renewed spirit—an insight, perception, sense, appreciation in relation to Divine matters—which is the work of the Holy Spirit. It is the faculty which makes its possessor assured in an inward way of what is of God and what is not so, when very fine questions are at issue and when things are not by any means obvious."[10]

Divine enablement follows divine understanding. The Spirit never gives us His will regarding any situation without giving His presence and power to enable us to follow through. The Holy Spirit works not only on the "wanter" but also on the "want to," the doing of that which He leads us to do (Phil 2:13). We do not have to be afraid to step out by faith. We can take the step of faith with the full assurance that the Holy Spirit will accompany us in the performance of His revealed will. (See chapter 10.)

A Christian man with unusual ability but also with unusual dependence upon the Holy Spirit within his spirit was called upon to fly out of the country to a ship where one of the large motors was having trouble. He was to locate and fix the problem. He inquired if there was another motor like it nearby, and he was informed that there was one in the States, but the company did not want him to waste time by stopping to see it. But he insisted on performing the task his way, which was the Lord's way. So it was agreed for him to stop to see the motor within the States. When he arrived at the site of the large motor which was properly functioning, he went in and examined it. Within fifteen minutes he had found the answer. The answer was wired to the people having difficulty with the repair of the motor. Soon the motor was repaired. How did this man do it? He depended on the Holy Spirit within to reveal to him the problem. The Holy Spirit took the man's training and revealed to him the cause of the problem. His walking in the Spirit made certain that this Christian's first diagnosis would be right.

The Holy Spirit is waiting to help us with our needs, problems, and decisions. Our need is to tune into Him, believe that He is present, and ask for His help. Trust Him to give His help, and act upon it when He does.[11]

9

Supernaturally Guided

God sometimes gives guidance through the supernatural or miraculous. It is granted that these are the exceptions, but they must be studied by those who would know the ways that God reveals His will.

God chose to give guidance to a medical doctor by miraculously healing him of cancer. His life has been committed to God ever since as a Spirit-filled, dedicated, and consecrated physician whose aim is to please the Lord Jesus as Jesus pleased the Heavenly Father (John 8:29).

In the story of Peter and Cornelius (Acts 10:1 to 11:18), God used two visions in two different places to bring the two together, so one could present the gospel and the other receive the gospel. Supernatural guidance is given so that people might do the will of God.

Biblically Exemplified

Supernatural guidance may be found throughout the Bible. God just makes an appearance through a supernatural being or sets aside His laws of nature to get through to His people in order to give a message to one or more of them.

Joseph was given supernatural guidance through God's

direct intervention in his life. Being despised by his brothers, Joseph was sold into slavery and eventually became second in command in all of Egypt. From this exalted position, he led the Egyptians to save their crops during their seven years of plenty, so they would have enough during their seven years of crop failure. When the food was diminished in Israel, the family of Joseph had to go to Egypt to buy food. This situation led to a confrontation between Joseph and his brothers. When the brothers learned that their benefactor was Joseph, their brother, they became very repentant. Then Joseph spoke up and said, "God sent me before you to preserve you a posterity in the earth, and to save your lives by a great deliverance. So now it was not you that sent me hither, but God" (Gen. 45:7-8). When the entire family had been brought into Egypt, Joseph said again, "Fear not: for am I in the place of God? But as for you, ye thought evil against me; but God meant it unto good, to bring to pass, as it is this day, to save much people alive" (Gen. 50:19-20).

Through the direct intervention in the life of Joseph, God had given guidance to him until Joseph became the savior of his people. Sometimes the going may look rough. It may appear that God is nowhere to be found, but He is there. And when you get to the end and look back, you will discover that His hand was on you every step of the way for a greater purpose.

Footprints

One night a man had a dream. He dreamed he was walking along the beach with the Lord. Across the sky flashed scenes from his life. For each scene he noticed two sets of footprints in the sand—one belonging to him, and the other to the Lord.

When the last scene of his life flashed before him, he looked back at the footprints in the sand. He noticed that many times along the path of his life there was only one set of footprints. He also noticed that it happened at the very lowest and saddest times in his life.

This really bothered him and he questioned the Lord about it. "Lord, you said that once I decided to follow You, You'd walk with me all the way. But I have noticed that during the most troublesome times in my life there is only one set of footprints. I don't understand why when I needed You most You would leave me."

The Lord replied, "My precious, precious child, I love you and I would never leave you. During your times of trial and suffering, when you see only one set of footprints, it was then that
                          I carried you."
                                        —Author Unknown

Nature's Elements

God chose to give directions to Moses and the children of Israel through a manifestation of the supernatural in nature's elements. As they marched through the wilderness, "And the Lord went before them by day in a pillar of a cloud, to lead them the way; and by night in a pillar of fire, to give them light; to go by day and night" (Ex. 13:21). The Wise Men were led to the place where Jesus was born by following a special star (Matt. 2:9-10).

God used an animal to stop Balaam from disobeying him. He placed an angel in the path of the donkey. Finally, the donkey spoke to Balaam (Num. 22:28-30). Balak wanted Balaam to defy Israel and curse Jacob and to bless Balak, but Balaam did the opposite because he had to obey the will of the Lord. Today, animals may not be used to speak audibly, but God can work through animals to reveal His will and direction to people if that be His desire. Dogs and cats have warned their owners of dangerous home fires in time for all to escape.

Many times God gave guidance to His people through the prophets. Often the prophets said, "The word of the Lord came unto me saying," "Thus saith the Lord," and "The Spirit of the Lord God is upon me." Even though the Bible does not say how the word of the Lord came or how the prophets knew that it was the Lord who spoke, they knew, and thus they spoke it and wrote it down for all to read as Isaiah, Jeremiah, Ezekiel, Daniel, and the twelve minor prophets. Then God had His speaking prophets to give guidance as Micaiah, Elijah, Elisha, and Nathan. Today, God has prophets to speak forthrightly His message to a sinful nation and world. We had better heed the message when God is speaking.

Angels were used of God to convey a message to His people much more than one would expect. An angel appeared to Hagar to inform her that she was to be the mother of Ishmael. Angels often came to Abraham to give guidance when God had no other method to communicate with him personally without appearing Himself. Lot and his family were literally yanked out of Sodom and Gomorrah by angels.

In the New Testament, several angelic appearances were manifested to Mary, Joseph, Zacharias, and the shepherds regarding the birth of Jesus. Peter had an angel to release him from jail. Paul had an angel to assure him that no lives would be lost during an impending shipwreck if all obeyed the orders given by the angel (Acts 27:23).

Angels have been known to make their presence visible on earth to communicate to God's people. A geologist was saved because he saw an angel nudging a turtle out of a dry creek bed. It seems he had heard that turtles could be seen leaving dry creek beds a few days before a flood. He wondered why. Being unsaved, he told the Lord if He would show him how the turtles knew to leave the creek beds, he'd believe in Him as His personal Savior and Lord. A few weeks later, the geologist was in the fields again and saw the turtles moving slowly up the hillside. Then, suddenly, he saw beyond space, and there was an angel with a stick nudging the turtle along. Unusual? Yes, but that man is a Christian today.[1]

A woman heard me tell this story about the angel nudging the turtle. When one of her two dogs ran off and became lost for several hours, she went into her prayer closet, obeyed the Scripture, and thanked the Lord for the situation. Then the Lord reminded her of the story regarding the turtle and revealed to her that He is all knowing and that He knew where the little dog was. So she said, "Lord, I know that You know where my little dog is, and You can bring her back home." She continued to worship, pray, and trust the Lord for the dog to return. While she was still praying, her son came home with the dog. Their second dog had been taken on a leash to the place where the first little dog was last seen. He pulled free from the young boy and went into a large brush pile and brought the little dog out. Supernatural? She thinks so.[2]

God sometimes chooses to give guidance through dreams and visions. Jacob saw a ladder and angels in his dream and accepted this dream as a promise of God for a large family. Joseph had dreams that foretold the future. Gideon discovered God's will through another person's dream. Daniel received the interpretation of Nebuchadnezzar's dreams through his own dreams. The Wise Men, after finding the baby Jesus, went back to their home another way because they were "warned of God in a dream that they should not return to Herod" (Matt. 2:12).

Peter quoted Joel as saying, "Your sons and your daughters shall prophesy and your young men shall see visions, and your old men shall dream dreams" (Acts 2:17). In a vision, Paul heard the Macedonian call, "Come over into Macedonia, and help us" (Acts 16:9). While praying and in a trance, Paul was told by the Lord to get out of Jerusalem.

According to the Bible and the testimony of some people, God has given directions and guidance through an audible word. David often sought directions from the Lord regarding the many battles he faced. When he was at Rephaim, the Philistines attacked again. When he inquired of the Lord, he was told not to go up until he heard "the sound of a going in the tops of the mulberry trees" (2 Sam. 5:24). Upon obeying the instruction, David waited until he heard, and then he went out and won the victory. On the Dasmascus road, Paul heard God speak in an audible voice. Being convicted by such a confrontation, he surrendered to the Lord Jesus Christ as Savior and Lord.

One woman heard the voice of God in the sound of the wind. In the voice were simple instructions to trust God for her need.

Humanly Unsought

In most of the biblical illustrations of supernatural guidance, the recipients of such guidance had not asked for it. In fact, supernatural guidance does not have to be sought. It is just a matter of continuing to live your life on a high spiritual level. God is not interested in making you a super saint so you can have some supernatural experience to share as you move along on your super-spiritual highway alone.

When Peter received his supernatural vision, he was not looking for it, nor had he asked for it. Peter was perfectly satisfied as he was, but God had an unsaved man and his family ready and waiting to be saved (Acts 10:9-23).

One may also note that this supernatural guidance usually comes during the day-by-day events of life. Peter was resting on the flat roof of his host's house. He was sleeping when God broke through to him. The shepherds were tending their sheep when the angels appeared to lead them to the birthplace of Jesus. Zacharias was tending to his temple duties when an angel appeared to him and said that his wife, who was "well stricken" in years, would give birth to a baby. David was tending the sheep. Samuel was assisting Eli in the Temple.

God has a way of changing directions for us through the supernatural as well as preventing us from going in the wrong direction (Acts 16:6).

Divinely Given

Peter received directions from the Lord through his vision. Peter's mind had to be changed. For many reasons he could not see the salvation of the Gentiles, but when God had finished with Peter, he was ready to include the Gentiles in God's redemptive plan. Peter's willingness to share with the Gentiles was a drastic departure from the belief of most of the Jewish Christians.

Such supernatural guidance is based upon two factors: God's sovereignty and human need. God knows everything that there is to know. His wisdom is superior to human wisdom. It is God's choice to use the miraculous. He doesn't have to have a reason or give a reason. Humans see from a small perspective; God sees everything from His total perspective.

But God takes into consideration human need. He knows where persons are and thus His wisdom never omits a lack of human wisdom. Some things would never dawn upon human hearts unless God intervened. And there are some things too precious and too needful in this world to wait until the human race is ready. There must be a supernatural breakthrough. And when such a need exists, God knows how to meet the need head-on in a supernatural way.

God is the Giver. Humanity is the receiver. Time was of the essence in regard to the inclusion of the Gentiles in God's plan of redemption being made known; so God acted then as He acts now.

Obviously Directed

There could be no doubt as to what God had in mind in giving Peter the vision. God's plan was obvious. Peter was to witness to the Gentiles. He was ready to learn the way. The truth that "God is no respecter of persons" must become known or must be brought out in the open (Acts 10:34). What better person through whom to make known this truth than Peter, a Jew. This witnessing confrontation would break down the walls of prejudice that had been built up over the centuries. It was time to move. Jesus had died, been buried, and was now resurrected. God was now ready to reach the world for Jesus.

Many other times God moved in supernaturally to convey a truth, give a command, or present a directive. What God was doing with Peter was obvious. When God gives supernatural guidance, it will be obvious to us. This guidance will not be missed.

In his vision, Peter could not have missed the point God was making. The vision was too clear. In Peter's vision was a sheet filled with things to eat, some of which Peter felt he could not eat because of his religious background. When Cornelius's men appeared at the door looking for him, Peter had no alternative; he had to go. Two impossible situations were about to meet at the foot of the cross.

Zacharias couldn't have missed the point when the message of God was embodied in an angel standing before him even though he still asked for a sign. The Wise Men could not have missed the place where Jesus was because the star of Bethlehem was hovering over it.

God may choose to reveal His directions to us in some miraculous manner, but we must believe in the miraculous as well as expect the miraculous. One thing is certain: we must not request it. But if we believe the miraculous, then we will believe the Bible. If we believe the Bible, we'll receive guidance from a study of the content of the Book. Embedded in the content there is a message for everyone of us. When we learn that message, we are well on our way to knowing and doing the will of God.

When God gives supernatural guidance, it must be obeyed. For it is His will, period. And we will obey if we are committed to God and to His ways and are sensitive to God's communication with us. Often God's simple will for us is to obey: children to parents, employees to employers, students to institutional leaders, local body of believers to spiritual authority, and all to God. Peter obeyed this supernatural guidance to witness to Cornelius. And God's hand was upon him.

Most of us will not hear an audible voice or see an

obvious miraculous manifestation of God's guidance, but all of us may find guidance in the Bible, through prayer, or through one of the methods of determining the will of God for our lives. If we seek supernatural guidance only, we'll miss the great spiritual enrichment that comes from intimate fellowship with the Holy Spirit and the Word of God. Elijah heard only a still small voice (1 Kings 19:12).

Many times God has reminded us suddenly concerning His will or what's best for us, but we have missed it because we were not expecting such an obvious reminder.

Recently, I had laryngitis, so each day I was taking four antibiotics and two antihistamines. I changed antihistamines, and for two nights I couldn't sleep. The antihistamines and antibiotics had mixed to become a stimulant. (In my previous reading I had been made aware that a mixture could occur.) I was wide awake and unable to sleep. Suddenly, I was reminded that some antihistamines would cause such a reaction and returned to my original ones. Did this change work? Of course, it did. The Lord was the One who had reminded me. And why should He make a mistake?

Sometimes we've been driving down the road and suddenly remembered something we needed to do. We acted accordingly and prevented a disaster. Who reminded us? Of course, the living Lord did. We need to thank Him for His reminders, if we have not done so already.

One night I was coming in from visitation. As I approached a heavily traveled street with a green light showing, I had a deep impression to slow down, even though I had a green light, and to approach the crossing of the street cautiously. So I obeyed my impression. Just as I approached the intersection, the driver of a large car came speeding through the red light. He either could not or did not stop. Had I not slowed down in my small car, I would have been hit and probably seriously injured. Coincidental? No, God was doing His work, and I was obeying. Praise the Lord!

A pastor was out visiting one afternoon. He thought of a family that he should stop by to see even though that family was not on his list. He obeyed, stopped, and knocked on the door. A woman came to the door. He gave a word of encouragement and an invitation to the church services and went on his way. That evening the telephone rang. It was that same woman, the one that he had been reminded to stop by and visit. She had planned to take her own life, but his visit had given her new hope. Coincidental? No, God was doing His work and His man was obeying.

10

Understanding the Will of Purpose

God had a deliberate purpose for all He did in the Old and New Testaments as He has a purpose for what He is doing today. This will of God is purposeful, deliberate, intelligent, gracious, elective, and redemptive. Whatever God purposes will come to pass. Some refer to God's will of purpose as God's sovereign will.

A study of the uses of the will of God reveals that 71 of the 122 occurrences of the will of God in the New Testament refer to the will of God as purposeful while the will of God as desire occurs 52 times in the New Testament. This difference is true in the Old Testament as well.

An examination of the term *the will of God* as it relates to purpose, according to the New Testament teachings, will enable us to understand the purposeful will of God. Then the distinction becomes obvious; God has a will that is preceded by deliberation and purpose. Thus, He knows beforehand what He is doing as He deliberates, plans, and then purposes. There are some things that God does and is going to do because He is God. He is going to do them whether we pray to Him, believe Him, or are interested in Him. He purposes to do these things independently of anything we do, feel, or think. God has reasons; sometimes we know them, and sometimes we don't. But whatever God purposes to do or does is right. Because God is who He is, everything He purposes to do or does has to be right. Do not be disappointed because all the great fundamentals of the faith are not mentioned in the phrase *will of God*. If these fundamentals are a part of the Bible, then they are within the total framework of God's ultimate plans and purposes. The Bible in its totality was and is the Word of God.

What a joy it is to know that we the redeemed are an exciting part of God's purposes. Such joy ought to drive us to the Word of God until we know not only what God's great purposes are but also what we already have. Our salvation had its beginning at conversion, but was planned before the foundation of the world. What a God! Better still, what a Savior! Little insignificant people as we are a part of the biggest plan of the universe. Hallelujah! The purpose of God may be noted in the following great concepts.

Creation

The purpose of God includes the creation. God thought, deliberated, planned, purposed, and acted. And we have the creation.

One minister said it well when he spoke of the creation: "God took a handful of nothing and threw it out into His created space, and from that nothing, there came into existence something."

The writer of Genesis described it better: "In the beginning God created the heavens and the earth."[1] One can't help recall the astronaut who read from space the first verses of Genesis. Hearing the Scripture read from space was awesome. The great God of glory was allowing one of His creatures to recognize the vastness of His expanse.

In Revelation 4:11, John recorded the redeemed's song of creation which is directed as praise to God. In the interlude of praise to God (4:9-11), the praise is twofold. First, the four living creatures give glory, honor, and thanks to God who sits on His throne and reigns eternally. Second, the four and twenty elders, who represent the redeemed of both the Old and New Testaments, fall down before the throne of the eternal living God and worship Him. As the elders cast off their crowns before the thone, they say, "Thou art worthy, O Lord, to receive glory and honour and power: for thou hast created all things, and for thy pleasure they are and were created." God's creation was in existence in His purpose before the actual creation in time. God planned to create the world before He actually did create the world. This work of creation is the effecting of the infinite purpose of God. Little wonder then that the redeemed of the Lord will shout their praises to a God with such infinite power and purpose.

Christ Jesus

God's purpose can be seen in everything that Christ Jesus was and is, and in everything He did and does. The Bible leaves no doubt about the preexistence of Jesus (John 1:1-5). His birth, life, and ministry were all directed by a purposeful God. In the deliberative halls of eternity, the plan was made. Jesus would come, live, and die for the sins of the world. Everything had been planned, and everything would go according to the plan.

It was no accident that Jesus was born in a stable. The exalted One must become the lowly One, so He might again become the highly exalted One who could and would make intercession for those who had accepted Him as Savior and Lord. And what a price to pay: born in a stable, reared out of His native land, and rejected by His own people, all according to the plan of God.

At His baptism[2], His transfiguration,[3] and during His ministry,[4] the Father said, "This is my beloved Son, in whom I am well pleased" (Matt. 3:17). All of these Scriptures are an assertion to the fact that God the Father was well pleased with the Son. The title "Son" identifies Jesus as the messianic Son of God (Ps. 2:7), and the expression "in whom I am well pleased" identifies Jesus as the Suffering Servant (Isa. 42:1).

God's good pleasure decided once and for all that Jesus was the Savior. The verb denotes its timelessness. God placed His purpose, decision, and resolution in Jesus. As the Messiah He was to carry out the Father's redemptive plan. Jesus would be His satisfaction. Jesus' life completely vindicated His choice. The announcements at His baptism and transfiguration were made, not because the Father came to be well pleased at these times, as He was already pleased, but because He wanted others to hear and receive the Son.

A leper came to Jesus, beseeching Him and kneeling down to Him, and said, "If thou wilt, thou canst make me clean."[5] He was actively submitting to what Jesus might purpose or determine to do about his disease. Jesus, upon being moved with compassion toward the leper, touched him and said, "I will; be thou clean."[6] He purposed to heal him and did so.

In John 4:34 Jesus declared that His meat (spiritual nourishment) was to do the will of the Father who sent Him to finish His work. So completely was Jesus occupied in the accomplishment of His mission and work that these actually became His food. Jesus had come to do the great purpose that God had planned for Him.[7]

Christ Jesus moved to the cross according to the purpose and plan of God. He had to die. And in the garden of Gethsemane He submitted absolutely to the perfect will and purpose of the Father.[8] In the mind of God Christ had been slain from before the foundation of the world. His death was in the determinate counsel and foreknowledge of God (Acts 2:23). Christ's death was a part of a plan. Christ was to die, and die He would. His incarnation would be joined with His redemptive sacrifice for our sins (Heb. 10:10). His sacrifice would be adequate in fulfilling God's purpose.

Although the death of Jesus was in the plan of God, Peter still could accuse these men of a brutal murder. When the enemies of Jesus assembled to destroy Him, they, in this intended act of cruelty, would do what God's "counsel" had "determined before to be done" (Acts 4:-28). In carrying out their own wicked design, they did exactly what God had predetermined and purposed. God had "marked off beforehand once for all" that Jesus was to die. It can be said with finality that the instigators of Christ's death were carrying out what God had already purposed, although they were doing their own wicked act.

Redemption

The whole plan of redemption had its origin in the gracious purpose of God. The "purpose of God to save," said W. T. Conner, "finds its revelation and means of accomplishment in Jesus Christ."[9]

Without Christ there is no redemption, and His death to accomplish such was according to the will of God (Gal. 1:4). Christ voluntarily "gave himself for our sins, that he might deliver us from this present evil world." His motive was to save. Thus, the entire redeeming work of Christ was due to the gracious purpose of God.

The redemptive plan required a vicarious Redeemer, one who would take our place. It was the Father's good pleasure that in Christ all the fullness of Deity should dwell and through Christ all things should be reconciled unto Himself. The fact that God, through the redemptive work of the Son, reconciled all things unto Himself (Col. 1:20 *b*) further indicates God's purpose as gracious. God carries out the redemptive purpose by making peace through the blood of the cross (Col. 1:20 *a*). Hence, Christ is the Agent of the plan of reconciliation. He is the One who makes us right in the sight of God.

The death of Christ removed the difficulty, the sin barrier between God and humanity, so that God's righteousness could be vindicated. The removal of the sin problem was accomplished when God set forth Christ Jesus as our sin bearer on the cross (Rom. 3:25). God publicly displayed the Son on the cross before the whole world.

In Ephesians 1:3-14 Paul set forth the most profound statement in all the Bible to show with many words[10] about the will and purpose of God that God has worked out with absolute thoroughness His saving purpose and plan. In the context Paul was emphasizing the provision of redemption in Christ (v. 3-14). These verses constitute one sentence without a predicate. Yet this passage of Scripture contains eight verbs of divine redemptive activity. In this sentence Paul discussed the work of God the Father (vv. 3-6), the work of Christ the Son (vv. 7-12), and the work of the Holy Spirit (vv. 13-14) in the foreordained plan of redemption. God's saving activity is not so much a spontaneous outburst of His goodness in response to a situation He had not contemplated beforehand, but rather it is the deliberate expression of His good will in a situation known from eternity. God knew in advance people would need a Savior, so He had a Savior planned from the beginning.

God chose believers before the foundation of the world and foreordained them "unto the adoption of children by Jesus Christ to himself, according to the good pleasure of his will" (Eph. 1:5). The choosing is a personal act of God. Although He does not coerce, God surrounds certain ones with influences that are conducive to salvation, and He marks them off as sons in Jesus Christ for himself. His purpose to save is an expression of his unmerited favor "according to the good pleasure of his will." Thus, God works out in history what He purposed in eternity.

God has fully uncovered and made known to Christians "the mystery of his will, according to his good pleasure which he hath purposed in himself" (Eph. 1:9) (compare Col. 1:27). Thus, redemption is according to the unmerited favor which God made to abound in all spiritual comprehension and practical discernment. Redemption is a secret now open. All who believe can be saved. These words clearly teach that the whole plan of redemption had its origin in the gracious purpose of God.

This purpose of God is free and determined wholly by Himself. This determination and purpose to save are expressions of his love and unmerited favor. He took counsel and found reason why He should purpose the salvation of believers. All things (grace, redemption, the universe, inheritance, and foreordination) are worked out according to "the counsel of his own will" (Eph. 1:11). God is the One who thought, planned, and purposed our salvation.

From all eternity God has had His heart set upon His people for their good and has been working out His purposes of grace concerning them (2 Tim. 1:9). But there is nothing arbitrary in His purposes or actions and unloving in His attitude toward anyone. John 3:16 reveals that His love is universal. But God will not force anyone to believe. He did not plan salvation to be based upon coercion.

God's counsel or entire gospel plan of salvation is immutable (Heb. 6:17). God's plan of redemption is unchangeable because God has made it impossible for His promise to fail and because Jesus has already entered into heaven as our forerunner. Our God deals with us as He purposes (Rom. 9:19). No one can outmaneuver God. God knows what He has resolved and purposed. Often a person blames God for his sin and pleads his rights against God. Yet God is never to be blamed. He has a right to deal with us as He finds us and as He purposes.

Jesus himself said that He "quickeneth whom he will" (John 5:21). And this power to give life to whom He wills is connected with and dependent on His power to judge (John 5:22). Thus, He gives life to whom He purposes, yet He purposes to give life to those that believe.

One can glory in the new assurance that redemption works in the realm of providence. God's loving providence takes care of those who love Him and who are the called according to His purpose (Rom. 8:28). Those who have continuously given God first place and have enthroned Him as the preeminent one are those for whom all things work together for good. The word *called* refers to God's drawing of the individual. God's dealing with the hearts of people results in their coming to Christ and being saved. This call is based upon God's deliberate purpose as He has a plan in regard to all who become believers, and this is not guesswork on His part. His sovereignty is behind all human freedom. The "good" works toward making believers conformable to Christ in spiritual character.

Christians are urged to carry out their salvation to completion with fear and trembling because God works in them "both to will and to do of his good pleasure" (Phil. 2:13). God purposes, initiates, and provides the power to realize the good in them. There is no higher principle of rightness than God's good pleasure by which He directs the lives of Christians. God's work is not finished until believers work out what God energizes in them. God's divine intention will be ultimately realized.

Human responsibility is seen in verse 12 and divine enablement in verse 13 (Phil. 2). Here, therefore, is the mysterious interaction between human freedom and the sovereign grace of God. For Paul there is no conflict between the two. Both human responsibility and divine enablement are a complement of each other. "Paul gives the divine sovereignty as the reason or ground for the human free agency."[11]

God deliberately chose Jacob and not Esau, and, in its implied sense, salvation is according to the elective purpose of God in Christ (Rom. 9:11). Since God is sovereign and purposeful, a person has no right to complain about God's actions in saving people even though one may not understand those actions.

Both Jews and Gentiles are partakers of the blessing of redemption, and the redeemed are the instruments used of God in making known this truth which is in accord with the eternal purpose of God (Eph. 3:11). Redemption for all has been a part of the plan and purpose of God from eternity. God never designed that only one race should partake in the redemption which He planned and provided by Christ. Salvation was for all the world. This redemptive plan and the method of its revelation were contemplated in God's eternal purpose and took place in accordance with that purpose. God's purpose has stood during the ages, and it was conceived and executed in and through Christ.

Believers become the first fruits of God's redemptive plan and thus become the heralds of this plan (Jas. 1:18). Thus, a person may be bold in enduring the hardships which may be caused by the preaching of the gospel. For such boldness and endurance one can rely upon the power of God who has provided salvation through Christ Jesus according to His own purpose (2 Tim. 1:9).

God considered the state of the world as He determined His gracious plan of redemption (1 Cor. 1:21). This plan included the "foolishness of preaching." "Preaching" refers to the content of the message, that which is preached. The idea of being made a new creature through the death of another person is foolishness to some. Yet preaching is the very medium through which God is pleased to save those who believe. To save them that believe is the heart of God's redemptive plan. God is pleased to save through the death of Christ on the cross.

As one person said, God elected to save some, and He also elected the means of their salvation which is by the proclamation of the good news. Election and missionary effort go hand in hand across a world for which Christ died.

In Special Calling

God has a special call and plan for some people. This plan is seen in a study of the calling and activities of the apostle Paul. God's unmerited favor was responsible for His separation and His call. His gracious purpose, which was seen in Paul's birth, came to its fulfillment in Paul's personal call. Even before Paul's birth God had His plans for Paul and called him (Gal. 1:15-16). The purpose of this revelation to Paul was that He might preach to the Gentiles as God purposed to make Paul an apostle to the Gentiles. In Paul's mind there was no doubt about His call.

Claiming to be called, Paul remarked that He was "an apostle of Jesus Christ through the will of God."[12] He became an apostle by an immediate call from Christ. The phrase "through the will of God" defines Paul's apostleship as coming by direct divine call and appointment. He felt God's purpose for him and welcomed it. He would be the first to say that he did not come into his apostleship by chance, or by growth, but through the underserved providence of God. In 2 Timothy 1:1, Paul said also that the will which made him an apostle was in accord with God's promise. He further stated that his apostleship was bestowed upon him by the grace of God (Eph. 3:7-8). In Titus 1:3 Paul said that he was intrusted with the message "according to the commandment of God our Saviour." In God's message to Ananias, Paul is declared to be a "chosen vessel" [vessel of election] (Acts 9:15).

In Acts 22:14 Paul speaks of his call and says that God appointed him to "know his will." He is quoting the words that were spoken to him by Ananias when Paul was in Damascus receiving the commission of God. Long in advance of this time God had determined that Paul was to know what God's will contained. Thus, Paul could say that he proclaimed the whole counsel of God (Acts 20:27).

Paul's activities were in accordance with the will of God. His trip into enemy territory would be God's plan for him (Acts 21:14). He prayed that he might be prospered by the will of God to visit the Roman church (Rom.

1:10). He was waiting for the divine decision. Also, he requested the church to pray that he might be able to visit them "by the will of God" (Rom. 15:32). The purpose of God for which Paul had been praying came to a reality when God spoke and told Paul that he wanted him to "bear witness also at Rome" (Acts 23:11).

Such a special call brought Paul to the place where he believed that his apostleship and his activities were based upon the purpose of God. Paul's walk with God verified that God had a purpose and a plan for him. That walk ought to be the pattern for every God-called servant.

Distribution of Spiritual Gifts

All spiritual gifts are derived from one Spirit and are given "to every man severally as he will" (1 Cor. 12:11). In the context Paul was discussing the diversity and unity of spiritual gifts (vv. 4-11). There is a diversity in them because there are nine different manifestations of the Holy Spirit. There is unity in them because the Spirit distributes them according to His purpose. This passage indicates that the Spirit is the worker because God works His purpose by the Spirit. The gifts are bestowed out of the sovereignty of God, out of His choice and judgment, according to His deliberate purpose.

God purposes and determines the various gifts for the individual members of the body of Christ (1 Cor. 12:18). Paul, in the midst of his illustration concerning the physical organs of the body, declared that God has "set the members each one of them in the body, even as it pleased him" (ASV). God has set the physical organs in the body according to His purpose. God's creative act had taken place in the past. Now His determining will has acted also. God has made the spiritual body to consist of many members even as He purposed it. By way of analogy Paul was saying that the members of the church have various functions and are set in their several offices and places according to the purpose and plan of God.

God bears witness to our great salvation or deliverance by the gifts of the Holy Spirit, according to His will (Heb. 2:4). This distribution of spiritual gifts is according to the sovereign will of God. It was according to His purpose and plan that He distributed the gifts of the Holy Spirit. Therefore, whatever our spiritual gift may be, it has come from a sovereign God who has deliberately chosen to give the gift to us. This gift cannot be caught or taught; it can only be cultivated.

Prayer

Believers are taught to pray according to the purpose and plan of God. Even though they may not know the whole scope of God's plan and purpose concerning the world and themselves, they may pray for its accomplishment.

In the Model Prayer Jesus taught that one should pray to the Father, "Thy kingdom come. Thy will be done in earth, as it is in heaven" (Matt. 6:10). This prayer calls for an attitude of submission to God. *Kingdom* is used here to express the rightful completeness of the authority of God in human affairs. The phrase *Thy will be done* is used to express absolute authority. The Kingdom does not come until His will is done. The reign of God means the will of God is being carried out. Prayer is to be one for the full accomplishment of God's purpose.

The purpose of the Father is to give the Kingdom to the believers as they abandon earthly interests (Luke 12:32).

Their Father's good pleasure is to give the Kingdom to them; thus, they are assured of it.

The followers of the Lord may have boldness in prayer because God hears them when they "ask any thing according to his will" (1 John 5:14). In the context John was saying that Christians may have knowledge of God's divine will. As God gives assurance of eternal salvation, He gives the further assurance of answered prayer. But if prayers are to be heard, they must be prayed according to God's will. If Christians recognize His will as the sum of all good, then God will give heed. Since the emphasis here is on particular petitions (v. 16), the desires of the ones praying must be in submission to God's purposes. A desire for that which is outside the purpose of God must die.

The passage implies that if believers do not pray according to God's purpose, then God will not hear them. Yet believers may or may not pray according to what God purposes for them. Prevailing prayer will meet the purpose of God. Too often the problem is unoffered prayers and undirected prayers instead of unanswered prayers.

Resurrection

The resurrection is promised by Jesus to all who truly believe in the Lord Jesus Christ (John 6:40). The Father purposes to save everyone who believes in Him and promises to raise the believer "at the last day." And this promise of the resurrection at the consummation of Christ's mission must be taken as the Father's purpose. Paul, in illustrating the nature of the resurrected body by noting the difference between the seed and the mature plant, stated that God gives the seed a body "as it hath pleased him, and to every seed his own body" (1 Cor.

15:38). God, the Giver of life, responds to the sower's trust by giving to the seed the body originally designed for it from creation. A body was given to the seed in accordance with God's past decree in creation by which the propagation of life on earth was determined from the beginning. The purposeful will of God is the efficient link between the seed and the plant. By way of analogy Paul was saying that each individual will receive an acceptable, resurrected body for his redeemed nature according to the determined purpose of God. Just as the seed receives a body of its own, so will the redeemed receive a changed body according to God's purpose.

One can see that God has a purpose and plan which cannot be thwarted by humankind or Satan. God deliberated upon some things, thought them through, planned them out, and then willed or purposed them. There will be no deviation on His part. He will not change.

Let us search the Scriptures and learn what God has purposed, accept the great unchangeables, get in on their joy, and bask in their glory. Such action will transform our lives and prepare us to obey the desires of His heart for us.

11

Discerning the Will of Desire

The Father's will is often related to His desire when a person's response and freedom are taken into consideration. If a person can say no to God's will or can disobey His will, then it could not be God's purposeful will. God's will of purpose is unchangeable. The Father will not force. He will not coerce. God's will, as noted in the Bible, often relates to what He wants for us and from us but is contingent upon our obedience.

God had a will of purpose for the children of Israel long before they came out of the Egyptian bondage into the wilderness. Israel was the chosen race. He would some day give through her lineage His Son, the Messiah. God's will of desire for the ones twenty years of age and above was that they might obey and march into the Promised Land and be His people, but they disobeyed and refused to go. As a result, all those twenty years of age and older except two died in the wilderness. Even Moses missed out on entering the new land because he had sinned. It is the desire of God for all believers to enter the victorious land called the victorious life. Too often many people make the decision to stay out. Were it God's will of purpose, believers would have to go into the victorious life. But since believers refuse to enter into their victory, God's will has to be His will of desire.

Jesus had a will of desire. This will is often seen in His life on earth. This will is used in the New Testament in the words spoken by the writers concerning Jesus, in the words spoken by others to Jesus, and in the words spoken by Jesus Himself. Here are some examples.

After going up into the mountain, Jesus called unto Himself those whom He desired, and they went to Him (Mark 3:13). This call was to summon to Him the disciples whom He wanted in order to appoint the twelve apostles, and they responded in accord with Jesus' desire.

Jesus desired that no one should know what house He entered in the territory of Tyre and Sidon (Mark 7:24). On one occasion, Jesus desired that none know that He and His disciples were passing through Galilee (Mark 9:30). It was His desire that their route be kept secret so He would not be hindered by the multitudes.

The disciples of Jesus came to Him on the first day of the unleavened bread and said to Him, "Where wilt thou that we go and prepare that thou mayest eat the passover?" (Mark 14:12). They were inquiring where Jesus wished for them to prepare the Passover meal.

Jesus, seeing the hungry multitudes who had been with Him three days without food and being compassionate toward them, called His disciples to Him and said, "I will not send them away fasting, lest they faint in the way" (Matt. 15:32). Jesus desired not to send them away hungry.

Peter stated that He was ready to build three tabernacles on the mount of transfiguration if Jesus desired to have a longer stay (Matt. 17:4). Jesus desired to protect the people of Jerusalem from danger as a hen gathers her chickens under her wings for protection (Matt. 23:37).

When He tasted the wine mingled with gall that was given to him on the cross, "he would not drink" (Matt. 27:34). He had no desire to drink the wine and become stupefied.

James and John, upon seeing the people of a Samaritan village refuse to receive Jesus, said, "Lord, wilt thou that we command fire to come down from heaven, and consume them" (Luke 9:54). The disciples were asking if Jesus wished for them to destroy the people.

On another occasion, Jesus said to the disciples, "I am come to send fire on the earth; and what will I, if it be already kindled?" (Luke 12:49). Jesus was saying that He wished that burning enthusiasm were already kindled. He did not wish to walk in Judaea because the Jews sought to kill him (John 7:1). And He also said that Peter was not to be concerned if Jesus did desire that John tarry till He come again (John 21:22).

It must be noted also that Jesus' desire was to fit into the purpose of God so that as Jesus' will related to the Father, it became one and the same with the Father's. This desire is noted in His experience in the garden of Gethsemane. There Jesus prayed, "Father, if thou be willing, remove this cup from me: nevertheless not my will, but thine be done" (Luke 22:42). Jesus was saying, "Father, if in Thy counsel and purpose, there is some other way for Me to die, then remove the cup."[1] Jesus was praying to die some other way rather than at the hands of men.[2] The decision was left to the Father. Jesus, undoubtedly, was asking the Father to look into His plans to see if there were another way. He had come to die for people, yet the very people for whom He had come to die were about to put Him to death. Such an act would make them more guilty and less likely to repent and be converted.

But the word *nevertheless* left the decision to the Father. Jesus would stand fast on the Father's decision. Jesus, then, expressed perfect submission to the Father's purpose, saying, "Not My personal desire but Thy purpose be done."[3] Jesus resigned Himself to the whole purpose of God. He was resigned not just to God's purpose concerning His death but to His purpose in all things. Even though this desire of Jesus to die some other way could not alter the plan of God, Jesus was willing as always to submit Himself into the Father's purpose and plan for His life. And in every instance His will of desire fitted into God's perfect plan. Being one with the Father, their purposes were one and the same. And being one with the Father, their desires were one and the same.

It is my belief that this will of Jesus was one of desire because He could have refused to die on the cross. Had He refused, He would not have been the perfect sacrifice for our sins. If Jesus' will of desire fitted perfectly into the Father's purpose and plan, then does not the Father want us to obey His will of desire until we fit into His ultimate plan and purpose?

God's will of desire, which may be called His moral will, involves many relationships. This will may be obeyed, or it may not be. God gives us this choice, but to disobey His desire brings a penalty. We also become less than what God expects of us. There is to be no joy in failing to be what God wants.

God has an affectionate desire for the entire human race, and this desire has always been the heartbeat of God. When Jesus was born, the angel and a multitude of the heavenly host declared that all people are the recipients of God's good pleasure. As the angel finished the announcement of the birth of the Savior to the shepherds, the heavenly host appeared praising God and saying, "Glory to God in the highest, and on earth peace, good will toward men" (Luke 2:14). God's good pleasure had come to the world in the person of Jesus Christ. "Men" here does not mean just believers but the whole human race, contemplated as blessed in the birth of Christ. Thus, the birth of Jesus was a display of God's desire for every person to come to Him.

Salvation

God desires all to be saved. This is His will, but not all are saved as is well known. Paul, in urging Timothy and the church to pray for all people, said that God "will have all men to be saved, and to come unto the knowledge of the truth" (1 Tim. 2:4). Here Paul gave the motive for prayer concerning all people. Prayer for everyone is good and acceptable in God's sight, for He continually desires all to be saved. "God is, so far as His inclination or will is concerned, 'the Saviour of all men,' but actually, so far as we can affirm with certainty, 'of them that believe' (1 Tim. 4:10)."[4] God does not will the death of any but desires that all should be saved through repentance and faith. God's benevolent desire is for the salvation of all but only in accordance with His righteousness and, therefore, through their faith in the redemption provided in Christ. This salvation that God has provided may be accepted or rejected.

God is "not willing that any should perish, but that all should come to repentance" (2 Pet. 3:9). Peter was discussing the reason for the delay of the second coming of Christ. The arguments of the mockers who said that there was nothing to this whole promise of Christ's return were being refuted. Today, Jesus delays because God does not wish that any should perish. The explanation for His delay is found in the character and purpose of God. Time, whether it be brief or long, is a minor matter to God. He delays His coming in order that people may have time to repent and to accept the salvation He has provided.

This desire of God for none to perish and for all to be saved is seen in the Scriptures. In Ezekiel 18:23 and 33:11 it is stated that God has no pleasure in the death of the wicked. (Compare Rom. 8:32; 11:32; Titus 2:11). Jesus wept over Jerusalem because He desired her to come to Him for salvation and protection (Matt. 23:37). God does not desire the death of any person or that any should perish, but He does desire that all should come to repentance. It is implied that some will perish, but that is not God's desire. He wants all to be saved.

God has a desire to show His wrath on sin (Rom. 9:22). Yet He extends His mercy to the sinner so he may repent. God's desire to show wrath on sin is the spontaneous will of God which grows out of His character. A paraphrase is as follows:

> God, although desiring or wishing to display his wrath and to make known his power to punish sin, has through his longsuffering delayed and endured with those deserving of destruction.[5]

This passage offers an answer to the objection that God is unjust by showing how the sovereign God has restrained His wrath and power in accordance with His righteous and holy desire. God does not do anything whereby a person may accuse Him of being unjust, but rather He is responsible for all the mercies extended to anyone.

God desires a response from everyone. His desire is for

mercy and not sacrifice (Matt. 9:13; 12:7). He does not desire sacrifices and offerings for their own sake. These responses must represent a changed life coming from a broken and contrite spirit.

Jesus says that not everyone saying "Lord, Lord, shall enter into the kingdom of heaven; but he that doeth the will of my Father which is in heaven" (Matt. 7:21). Mere talkers or confessors will not be saved. The ones saved will be those doing the desire of the Father. What is this desire? God's desire is a belief in the Lord Jesus Christ that results in a changed life (2 Cor. 5:17). A changed life will cause one to do what God desires constantly. His life-style will show it.

Sanctification

God desires our sanctification. He wants us to grow into Christlikeness. It is His will that we do so. God has given us salvation through faith in Jesus Christ. He is to be our all. He is to be our constant companion and guide. We are to keep our face toward Him so we may be all that God intends. It is His will that we become like Christ (Rom. 8:29). God has placed within us the Holy Spirit, one like unto Jesus to glorify Jesus and to reveal Him unto us. He has surrounded us with everything that we need to grow and become Christlike in character—the Word of God, the church alive, the knowledge and the wisdom of God, fellow believers, and the challenge of the hour.

There are no shortcuts to maturity. No one emotional experience will get it.[6] Becoming mature is a lifetime work under the direction of God. Whatever God starts out to do He will accomplish (Phil 1:6). He will create within us a desire to be Christlike and will provide the energy for the accomplishment (Phil 2:13). He'll change our "wanter," make us want to do His will, and then will do it for us and through us.

Jesus wants to live out His life in and through us, but we have to permit Him to do so. We have to make ourselves available. Making ourselves available is where the will of desire dovetails with our growth into Christlikeness. Whatever Christ wants is His will, and He wants much from us. There is no getting around God's will of desire in relation to human responsibility. God demands us to do something, to be something. God's will demands a response, and that response is what causes His will in our sanctification or growth in Christlikeness to be His will of desire and not His will of purpose. Otherwise, every believer would be coerced by the sovereign God to respond in Christlike growth.

Life shows that the response to growth is different on the part of believers. Some respond quickly to every demand of the Father, and some respond slowly. But God is patient, and He waits upon us. God may prod us, spank us, challenge us, and urge us on, but the surrendered will is a must if we are to become Christlike. Only as we surrender will we go into the Word to learn about Christ Jesus and His way, spend time in prayer and fellowship with Him, or worship Him corporately and individually. For it is His desire to bring us to the place in our Christian lives that His ways are our ways, His thoughts are our thoughts, and His desires are our desires. "Delight thyself also in the Lord; and he shall give thee the desires of thine heart" (Ps. 37:4). The psalmist was not saying, "Give a glad hand to the Lord, and we'll get anything we want." The promise is to get the desires of our hearts when our hearts want only the Lord Himself. For when we have Him, we have everything we need.

God also has a will that relates to our responsibilities.

Morally Upright

That every believer be morally upright is God's desire. "For this is the will of God, even your sanctification, that ye should abstain from fornication" (1 Thess. 4:3). The word *this* states that the will of God is what follows—our "sanctification." We are to be consecrated and separated from sins, even the sins of a moral nature. Fornication and other sexual impurity are not within the will of God. What God wants is purity and growth into Christlikeness.

An understanding of what God desires is an imperative, not an option. We do not have a right to look at God's will and take up what we like as we would in a cafeteria line. "Wherefore be ye not unwise, but understanding what the will of the Lord is" (Eph. 5:17). Believers are urged to avoid senselessness because of the nature of the Christian walk. Such a walk requires the cultivation of wisdom and not folly. Being wise is a command to perceive that it is the Lord's will to live such a life as a Christian. The desire of the Lord is related primarily to the kind of living reflected in these verses (vv. 18-33). The Bible forbids us to get drunk, which causes a person to act foolishly, but are commanded to be filled with the Holy Spirit who controls us and guides us in proper conduct.

Doing the desire of God ought to be an object of our prayers. A concern for our conduct and the conduct of others will drive us to prayer. Nothing should keep one from praying. Our prayer ought to be that all believers may "be filled with the knowledge of his will in all wisdom and spiritual understanding" (Col. 1:9). God has a will that must be obeyed, and we need to discover it. We need convictions regarding the conduct that God requires.

Both the power to make the right choices and the ability to discover the real connection between the many events coming into one's life are necessary for an apprehension of God's will. He will make his will clear to us regarding the moral issues that we face. Being morally upright in our Christian walk is God's requirement.

Transformed Life

A transformed life is the desire of God. Believers must stop being fashioned according to the world and be transformed by the renewing of their mind so that they "may prove what is that good, and acceptable, and perfect, will of God" (Rom. 12:2). There are spiritual requirements for the saved. One is to present the body as a holy and acceptable sacrifice. As a result of this yielding to God, Christians are to stop allowing themselves to be molded by the world. They are to be made into a new person by a complete reversal in their way of thinking. Having one's thinking changed produces a complete transformation of character and life. Thus, Christians may discern in their experience what the will of God is. They may demonstrate the will of God. His will is what He desires. The renewed mind longs to discover what God desires, and only such a mind is able to do this. The content of that will is noted in the words *the good, acceptable,* and *perfect.* The will of God then is identified with what is morally good for Christians, with what is well pleasing to God, and with what is ethically complete in itself. Such a life will not be conformed to this world, but this life will cut across the grain. A transformed life is what God wants and expects. And we need to have such in our Christlikeness.

The goal of such transformation is found in the desire of God, too. It is that we may "stand perfect and complete in all the will of God" (Col. 4:12). The followers of Christ need to stand mature and fully assured. And it is in the sphere of the will of God that one may arrive at maturity and assurance. This standing fast is confined to the ethical life with which God's desire is concerned. So God's desire is that His followers may be changed into the likeness of His Son.

Complete Obedience

God's will calls for complete obedience to Him. Complete obedience is the goal of every believer and is the desire of the living Lord.

As an example of God's desire for obedience, one may look at David. The apostle Paul said that God had found "David the son of Jesse, a man after mine own heart, which shall fulfil all my will" (Acts 13:22). David, as compared with the disobedient Saul, was a man who faithfully obeyed the commands of God and who did the "wills"[7] of God in spite of his sins of which he repented. He was willing to do all the "wills" of God, that is all the different things that God desired for him to do.

Obedience to God is demanded in every area of life. Being a Christian gives us no excuse for failing to be a good worker on the domestic scene or failing to be a law-abiding citizen.

God's desire for the servants of Christ is to do "the will of God from the heart" (Eph. 6:6). Order in domestic life is expected and especially in the life of servants and masters or employee and employer. One is to serve one's master with fear and trembling and in sincerity (v. 5). The phrase "as unto Christ" is a Christian expression and demands that one conduct oneself as a Christian. Even though no one else may be looking, God is. Proper conduct should be a habit, nothing phony, for that is what God wants from every one of His followers. And this kind of obedience will be done with hearty readiness, if done according to the desire of God.

Christian citizens are to obey the law. "For so is the will of God, that with well-doing ye may put to silence the ignorance of foolish men" (1 Pet. 2:15). Obedience to the civil authorities is a virtue of the Christian life. Doing the right thing further explains what the will of the Lord is and describes the method of being submissive. It is God's desire that believers submit and be subject to the civil authorities, for such obedience results in quieting the slanderers, those who would attack the cause of Christ for the failure of Christian citizens.

The doing of God's desire is dependent upon the fashioning and perfecting of the believer in every good work. The prayer of all Christians ought to be: "[May God] Make [us] perfect in every good work to do his will, working in [us] that which is well-pleasing in his sight, through Jesus Christ; to whom be glory for ever and ever" (Heb. 13:21).[8]

When God brings us to a knowledge of his Son, then we are ready and able to do His will. God who could raise the Lord Jesus from the dead can furnish us with every good thing for the doing of His will. One can be equipped with whatever is necessary to the doing of His will. God continuously works in us through the Lord Jesus Christ that which is well pleasing in His sight, so we may be filled with the spirit of obedience.

Faithful Service

God wants more than our money; He wants us. When He has us, then He has our money and everything else over which we have been made trustee. Therefore, our time becomes His; our love becomes His; our selves become His. And our little-or-much material resources become His also. Thus, our lives should continually be epitomized by service.

The churches of Macedonia not only gave their money but went far beyond expectations in that they first surrendered themselves to the Lord in personal service and as laborers with Paul. This complete surrender was made "by the will of God" (2 Cor. 8:5). They gave themselves to the Lord and as laborers with Paul in response to God's desire. It was the divine desire to which the Macedonian churches had responded, and it was God's desire that the Corinthian church should respond in serving and in giving also.

Faithful service has as its source the desire of God who desires liberal gifts, complete surrender, and faithful commitment.

Continuously Thankful

Being thankful all of the time in every circumstance is not the easiest command to apply in our lives. Yet the Bible says, "In every thing give thanks: for this is the will of God in Christ Jesus concerning you" (1 Thess. 5:18). The duty of thanksgiving is the basic aspect of God's will, but rejoicing always and praying without ceasing may be included in the scope of His will also. Grateful praise is to be a continuous offering to God, for He desires this in every Christian. And this will of desire is operative and effective in Christ Jesus.

Bitterness and complaints would be eliminated from the life of the believer if this command to thank the Lord in everything were obeyed. Some say, "But, how can I thank the Lord for a flat tire, a broken arm, a trip to the hospital, or a big disappointment?" These are typical responses. The Bible says, "In everything give thanks." God didn't say "for everything good." "In everything" covers the good and the bad. In His teachings Jesus implied that the unsaved can be grateful for the good. So, if there is to be an impact for good and the cause of Christ, then it must come from the saved who will thank God for the bad circumstances of life. For it is in praise that power is released in our difficult circumstances, so God can bring good out of the difficult (Rom. 8:28).

Before you try to interpret the word *in*, search the Scriptures. Our Lord said through Paul, "Giving thanks always for all things unto God and the Father in the name of our Lord Jesus Christ" (Eph. 5:20). So give thanks for all things and in everything. Then watch Him release His power in you to help you through the difficulty. God is not a bridge over troubled waters, but He is a tunnel through troubled waters.

Persistent Endurance

Life is filled with trials and sufferings. Yet believers are encouraged to live the rest of their time on earth in spite of their trials according "to the will of God" (1 Pet. 4:2). Trials and sufferings can be endured because of the example of Christ and because of the indwelling Christ. As Paul said, "Christ in you, the hope of glory" (Col. 1:27). In order to be persistent in endurance, one must arm oneself with the same attitude of Christ (1 Pet. 4:1). "The word which is translated *attitude* is usually translated *mind* or *thought*. It means mental response."[9] The desire of God is that the outward life may be governed by the same principles of the inward life.

The realities of life must be faced now. That suffering

cannot be denied is a fact of life. And the Lord would have us to face our trials courageously and victoriously.

Christians need patience in order to receive the promise after doing "the will of God" (Heb. 10:36). Doing the will of God is an essential requirement for one to receive the promise. The doing of God's will is conditioned upon persistent endurance. Only the person of persistent faith can be victorious. Consistent daily living until the end is God's desire, and it can be done. There must be no turning back or giving up. The promise awaits. The Lord is going to come again. If the trials of life cannot be understood now, they can be understood at his coming. "Even so, come, Lord Jesus" (Rev. 22:20). In the meantime, let us keep on doing what God wants.

Abidingly Saved

What better way to prove that we are saved, that we have kinship to Jesus, and that we are abiding in Jesus, than to do the will of God? He tells us what His will is. He tells us what He wants to see and others to see in our Christian lives. Then He gives us His presence and power to do what He wants and adds that the doing of His will proves we are His children.

Jesus, in giving the definition of spiritual kinship, says, "Whosoever shall do the will of God, the same is my brother, and my sister, and mother" (Mark 3:35; compare Matt. 12:50). All those who do the Father's will are Jesus' spiritual relatives. Those who do the will of God are those who follow Christ and become one with Him.

The world is going to pass away. But there is an abiding quality to the believer who does "the will of God" (1 John 2:17). As an object of lust, the world continuously passes away in the sense that it offers nothing that is permanent on which to set the affections. But in the midst of transitory things, doing "the will of God" alone is permanent. "The man who lives to do the will of God, who makes the will of God the law of his life, finds life that is enduring."10 Doing what God desires must be a settled tendency and ruling characteristic in the Christian's life if one is to abide forever. Such conduct brings assurance to the believer.

Without assurance, there is ineffective service. And ineffectiveness on the part of God's little ones "is not the will of your Father" (Matt. 18:14). He does not desire that His little ones should lose their effectiveness in service. He desires effectiveness. So to be effective, one must do what God wants. Doing God's will requires the help of Jesus, who is always there. In fact, He will do for us all that He requires of us if we surrender to Him, or as Paul said, "Put . . . on the Lord Jesus Christ" (Rom. 13:14; compare Gal. 3:27).

In the prayer of our Lord just prior to His crucifixion, He prayed for all future believers. Jesus' prayer was an expression of His desire for our spiritual unity and for our continual presence with Him in His glory. This prayer has not come to pass, but one day it will. Read it again.

Father, I will that they also, whom thou hast given me, be with me where I am; that they may behold my glory, which thou has given me: for thou lovedst me before the foundation of the world (John 17:24).

12

Grasping the Will of Permission

A Christian couple's little boy, while riding his bicycle on the sidewalk in his community, was hit and killed by a drunken driver who could not keep his car in the street. Many questions faced the grief-stricken parents. And their questions face us today. Was this the will of God? The normal reply depends on what you mean by the will of God. Did God purpose the boy's death in such a manner? Did God want the boy's death to occur in such a way? To answer in the affirmative would mean to the average person that God is a murderer. Yet, no Bible-believing Christian believes that God is a murderer, nor that God has ever been involved in any situation that could classify Him as a murderer. So if God did not plan or desire the death of the boy, then the next question arises. Did God know about the death before it happened and as it happened? If God knows all, then God had to know about the impending accident as well as the actual death.

In his book, Morris Ashcraft gave similar thoughts in a discussion of the mystery of evil.[1] He referred to others who gave these alternatives as their answer to evil: "God would remove evil if He could; God is able to but is not willing to do so; He is neither willing nor able to do so; He is both willing and able to do so." He concluded that the last alternative is the only acceptable one to the Christian. But then Dr. Ashcraft stated that he thinks it better to avoid the permissive-will-of-God interpretation of God's will. He prefers not to say that God permits us to do wrong or suffer wrong, but that He gives freedom.[2]

God's Foreknowledge

God foreknows all things including free human acts, even the most wicked deeds. To deny such foreknowledge would mean that God does not know the future either. If the choices and activities of humankind cannot be known by God until after they have taken place, that leaves God knowing no more than we know. In effect, God would be trailing the procession rather than leading it.[3]

God's omniscience and His foreknowledge are emphasized in both the Old and New Testaments in many places. God said concerning Abraham, "For I know him" (Gen. 18:19). Paul declared, "O the depth of the riches both of the wisdom and knowledge of God! how unsearchable are his judgments, and his ways past finding out!" (Rom. 11:33). Regarding Israel, Paul said that "God hath not cast away his people which he forknew" (Rom. 11:2).

When Paul spoke of believers, he wrote: "For whom he did foreknow, he also did predestinate to be conformed to the image of his Son" (Rom. 8:29). Peter spoke of believers as being "Elect according to the foreknowledge of God the Father" (1 Pet. 1:2). In his sermon on the Day of Pentecost, Peter told of Christ who was "delivered by the determinate counsel and foreknowledge of God" to be crucified by sinful men (Acts 2:23). God's foreknowledge and human freedom were placed side by side by the apostle Peter. Even the apostle Paul tried the two concepts together when he was being escorted by ship to Rome to be tried before Caesar. Yet when the ship wrecked on the rocks of the island of Melita, Paul warned them that if any tried to leave the ship, then all would perish (Acts 27:31). Thus, to Paul the matter was fixed from God's point of view, yet contingent upon human obedience to God's command.

God's Laws

There are some things that God permits that may be good or may be bad because most of the time He permits His laws to function without His interference. This principle is called the natural operation of His laws. But out of such normal functioning of His laws, Paul said, God can and will bring good to the saved who love Him if they will allow Him to do so (Rom. 8:28-29). Even though the Lord may not have planned a trial that is headed in our direction, by the time it reaches us it has God's permission written on it, and He is ready to make it work for our good.

Law is God's method of working. The world is governed according to law, not by the law. Natural law is not a force but the statement of a method according to which power works. It is God who rules the world, not natural law. For natural law is God's method of working. Even though natural law works regularly, it is not necessarily invariable. For the power behind the law can and does transcend the natural law for God's purposes and human good. God could not carry out His benevolent purposes in a world that operated by chance. The regularity of the world's operation reveals the faithfulness of God in carrying out His purposes in the world.[4]

"The whole temporal order, including man and all his

activities, is grounded in the will of God."[5] And since God knows the entire world order, He knows it in its parts and even in its single events.

Let us not blame God when we must pay the price for our disobedience of His laws. One humorist said, "Those who go against the grain of God's laws shouldn't complain when they get splinters."

God's Permission

Thus, if God knows all and if He does not purpose or desire that some things occur, then the only explanation is that He permits those things to happen, good or bad.

T. B. Maston[6] was right when He said that a child who was left with brain damage as a result of a person's failure to regulate the temperature in an incubator comes under God's permissive will. God ordinarily permits His natural laws to function without interfering with them. If God chose to completely dominate the lives of all people, then they would become robots, would never learn how to protect themselves, and would not become mature followers of the Lord Jesus Christ.

Strange as it may seem, people accept this concept of God's permissive will until an unexplainable tragedy occurs. Then these same people revert to the cliché, "It's the will of God," not knowing what is being said and, in too many cases, not caring who is hurt.

Is tragedy the will of God? In the sense that God planned it or desired it, the answer would have to be no. The Bible does not teach that God is responsible for every tragic event. His foreknowledge of an event does not mean that He plans it to happen. Satan is presented as the source of much tragedy in the world. (See the Book of

Job.) The only part that God had in the tragedies of Job is that He did not perform a miracle to prevent them.

Satan tempts us through the tragedies of life whether they be caused by Him or by the normal or abnormal operation of the natural laws of God. He is ready to pounce on every tragedy in order to defeat us.

It was Satan who proposed that God put forth His hand to afflict Job (1:11). But God did not afflict Him. However, He permitted Satan to afflict Job in order to clear His character. Satan had slandered Job's character by saying that Job only served God for what he could get out of Him. God knew this was a lie, and Satan knew it was a lie. In Job we see the permissive will of God in that God permitted Satan to do some things to Job. Even Ashcraft admitted that there is a permissive will if the Book of Job is understood as "literal history."[7]

But Satan was not finished with Job. If Satan cannot get to a person in one area, then he will try another. So Satan suggested that Job cared for nothing or no one but himself (2:4). In other words, Satan was saying, "Every man has his price." But this idea is one of Satan's lies, too.

At first Satan was permitted to afflict Job by taking Job's property and destroying his children. Now God again refused to lay His hand on Job to afflict Him bodily, but He permitted Satan to afflict Job bodily but with limitations. Satan could not take Job's life (2:6). To prove us genuine, to develop us, and to strengthen us, God in His wisdom permits us to experience tragedies, whereas Satan seeks to prove us a phony or a weakling and to destroy us in those same tragedies.

Whenever our position in life looks hopeless, and the tragedies, trials, and testings continue to come, we can hang on to God's glorious promise:

> There hath no temptation [testing] taken you but such
> as is common to man: but God is faithful, who will not
> suffer [permit] you to be tempted above that ye are able;
> but will with the temptation also make a way to escape,
> that ye may be able to bear it (1 Cor. 10:13).

Paul, in speaking of his visiting the church at Corinth,
said, "But I will come to you shortly, if the Lord will, and
will know, not the speech of them which are puffed up,
but the power" (1 Cor. 4:19). The clause "if the Lord will"
refers the willing to the indeterminate time of the visit.
Paul would visit Corinth if God permitted. He based his
future visit on the permissive will of God. In 1 Corinthians
16:7, Paul said that he would tarry a while with them "if
the Lord permit." The permissive element is noted also
when Paul said that he would return to Ephesus, "if God
will" (Acts 18:21).

When the writer of Hebrews told the Christians to stop
going over the same elementary principles but to go on
into those teachings that would lead to maturity, he said
that he was going to teach them concepts that would
bring maturity "if God permit" (6:3).

In 1 Peter 3:17, Peter informed the recipients of his
letter that it is better to suffer, "if the will of God be so,"
for well-doing. Peter was concerned about Christians enduring the persecutions that might come from the pagans
and religious leaders. He was encouraging them to endure trials because of the occasion of the suffering (3:13-
17). The will of God here refers to possible suffering and
emphasizes the permissive will of God. Peter was emphasizing to Christians that they should patiently endure suffering because God is the One permitting it. (See 1 Pet.
4:19.)

James, in protesting against the avarice of the arrogant recipients, gave the proper attitude that they should have toward the future. This attitude is expressed in the words, "If the Lord will, we shall live, and do this, or that" (4:15). This condition expresses the proper attitude of the mind. "The Lord" is the One who has the power over all time. There is nothing uncertain to Him. The life and conduct of these recipients are dependent upon God's will. "This or that" covers not just future planning but everything that God may permit to be done.

There is more comfort in believing that our ten-day-old baby girl died as a result of human failure than believing that God planned or desired her death. God knew about her illness and death before the illness appeared. Thus, He permitted the laws of nature to work. Someone violated nature's laws, and a strep germ entered into her body through the area where the umbilical cord was cut. Through the difficult experience, God worked for our good. He gave my wife and me His presence. We were able to bear the emotional stress. We have been able to sympathize with many others and to minister to them in a similar sorrow. God's permissive will has been allowed to work its way through our lives many times since that sorrow. And God will do the same for everyone who will allow Him to do so.

Epilogue

Certainly there are other avenues of finding the will of God, such as godly counsel (Prov. 11:14; 19:20), providential circumstances (Rev. 3:7), spiritual gifts (Rom. 12:3-8), and so forth, that have not been explored in depth in this book. But it is the basic conviction of this author that a conscientious and dedicated Christian can find the will of God on any matter if he or she will use one or more of the procedures discussed in these chapters. It must be assumed by every genuine follower of the Lord Jesus and by every Bible student that God wants us to know His will. He does not seek to convey His will to us in such vague ways that we can't understand it. God wants us to know His will. He was not vague in setting forth that will to the people of the Bible. If God is not ambiguous in revealing His will in the Bible, He will not be obscure in revealing His will to us—regardless of our situations and circumstances.

Thus, we should search for the will of God with a belief that God is anxious and ready to reveal His will and way. If we are ready, God is ready, for He has been ready. He wants us as His children to obey Him and please Him so He can be well pleased with us.

Let us start obeying the truth as we know it. Our obedience will reveal how well we are doing God's will. And when it becomes necessary to use these practical steps in determing the will of God for a particular situation, it will be easy to do so.

A little girl came to Sunday School and church by bus. It wasn't long until she knew the will of God for her was to trust the Lord Jesus Christ as her Savior. But that is not the end of the story. The same Holy Spirit who convicted and led the little girl to accept Christ was guiding her to request baptism. She was asked, "What are you going to do if your father beats you for being baptized?" Her reply was sublime. She answered, "I'll crawl up in his lap, put my arms around his neck, and tell him I love him." Wow! That's knowing and doing the will of God.

Notes

Introduction

1. Brackets mine.

2. Brackets mine.

3. In case one wants to make a study of the words that relate to the will of God in the Bible, check the thesis of the author at the library of Southwestern Baptist Theological Seminary, Forth Worth, Texas, May 1951. It is entitled "The Will of God as Reflected in Greek Words," Even though there are four basic Greek words, the conclusion reached was that the four words were used interchangeably when referring to the will of God and shaded toward distinctiveness in the context only when dealing with the different aspects of His will. This distinctiveness is noted in the last three chapters of this book.

Chapter One

1. The couple has already completed several years of happy marriage.

2. Ron Dunn, "If Any Lack Wisdom" (tape).

3. See the chapter entitled "The Storm of the Holy Spirit's Ministry," Jerry L. Glisson, *The Church in a Storm* (Nashville: Broadman Press, 1983).

4. Mrs. Shirley Nails—personal experience.

Chapter Two

1. Jerry L. Glisson, *The Church in a Storm*, p. 159.

2. I would encourage those seeking a promise to read Psalms, Proverbs, or Isaiah 40—66.

3. Manley Beasley, *Adventures in Faith*, (Port Neches, Texas: Foundational Truth Publication, 1974), p. 15.

4. A. T. Robertson, *Word Pictures in the New Testament*, (Nashville: Sunday School Board of the SBC, 1931), Vol. IV, p. 213.

5. Manley Beasley, *op. cit.*, p. 31.

6. Manley Beasley, *The Reality of God,* (Euless, Texas: Priority Ministries, 1978), p. 35.

7. E. F. Hallock, "I Have Discovered the Way of Gladness" (Tape).

8. Brackets mine.

9. E. F. Hallock, "Walking by the Promises" (Tape).

10. Warren and Ruth Myers, *Discovering God's Will,* (Colorado Springs: Navpress, 1980), p. 103.

Chapter Three

1. Manley Beasley's illustration

2. My paraphrase.

3. Ibid.

4. Mrs. Coy Loden's personal experience.

Chapter Four

1. My paraphrase.

2. Manley Beasley, *The Reality of God,* p. 35f.

3. Ron Dunn, "How Christ Abides in You"; "How to Abide in Christ" (Tapes).

Chapter Five

1. William L. Blevins, *Care and Maintenance for the Christian Life* (Waco, Texas: Word Books, 1979), p. 106.

2. Ron Dunn, *The Faith Crisis* (Wheaton, Ill.: Tyndale House Publishers, 1984), p. 155. Used by permission.

Chapter Six

1. Manley Beasley with Ras Robinson, *Laws for Liberated Living Study Guide* (Fort Worth, Texas: Fulness House, Inc., 1980), p. 22.

2. Ron Dunn, *The Faith Crisis,* p. 45. Used by Permission.

3. Ibid., p. 47.

4. Read Ron Dunn's comments in *The Faith Crisis,* pp. 49-51.

5. Ibid., p. 51.

Chapter Seven

1. Warren and Ruth Myers, *Discovering God's Will,* p. 35.

2. Roy Hession, *The Calvary Road* (Fort Washington: Christian Literature Crusade, 1950), p. 22. Used by permission.

3. Warren and Ruth Myers, *Discovering God's Will*, p. 35.

4. Some of these ideas were delivered in a message at the Leawood Baptist Church, Memphis, Tennessee, by Peter Lord, "Knowing God's Voice" (tape).

5. Manley Beasley, n.p.n.

6. *The Modern Language Bible, The Berkeley Version in Modern English* (Grand Rapids, Mich.: Zondervan Publishing House, © 1945, 1959, 1969). Used by permission.

Chapter Eight

1. Leighton Ford, "Soul Power," *Decision*, Mar. 1971, p. 4.

2. Brackets mine.

3. Brackets mine.

4. Brackets mine.

5. F. B. Meyer, *Directory of the Devout Life* (Grand Rapids, Mich.: Baker Book House, 1954), pp. 61-62.

6. J. Stafford Wright, *Man in the Process of Time* (Grand Rapids, Mich.: Wm. B. Eerdmans Publishing Co., 1956), p. 152.

7. Major W. Ian Thomas, *The Mystery of Godliness* (Grand Rapids, Mich.: Zondervan Publishing House, 1964), p. 53. Used by permission.

8. Ibid., p. 90.

9. T. Austin-Sparks, *What is Man?* (Indianapolis: Premium Literature, n.d.), p. 92.

10. Ibid., p. 93.

11. Thanks to Herb Hodges for permitting the use of his manuscript entitled "Man—His Nature, His Fall, and His Salvation" as background material for this chapter.

Chapter Nine

1. Story told in a Bible Conference in Memphis, Tennessee.

2. Mrs. Isabelle Keathley's experience.

Chapter Ten

1. This is my translation from the Hebrew text of Genesis 1:1.

2. Mark 1:11; Matthew 3:17; 12:18; Luke 3:22.

3. Matthew 17:5; 2 Peter 1:17.

4. Matthew 12:18.

5. Mark 1:40; Matthew 8:2; Luke 5:12.

6. Mark 1:41; Matthew 8:3; Luke 5:13.

7. John 5:30; 6:38,39; 11:4; 12:49,50; 14:31; 15:10; 17:4.

8. Matthew 26:42; Luke 22:42.

9. W. T. Conner, *Christian Doctrine* (Nashville: Broadman Press, 1937), p. 169.

10. All of the four basic Greek words for will of God are used in this passage of Scripture: counsel, will, good pleasure, and purpose.

11. A. T. Robertson, *Paul's Joy in Christ* (New York: Fleming H. Revell Company, 1917), p. 146.

12. 1 Corinthians 1:1, 2 Corinthians 1:1, Colossians 1:1, Ephesians 1:1, 2 Timothy 1:1.

Chapter Eleven

1. This is a paraphrase of the passage.

2. Andrew M. Fairbairn, *The Philosophy of the Christian Religion* (New York: The MacMillan Company, 1947), pp. 425-433.

3. This is a paraphrase of the passage.

4. Newport J. D. White, *The First and Second Epistles to Timothy and the Epistle to Titus,* The Expositor's Greek Testament (Grand Rapids, Mich.: Wm. B. Eerdmans Publishing Company, n.d.), p. 104.

5. Marvin R. Vincent, *The Epistles of Paul, Word Studies in the New Testament* (Grand Rapids., Mich.: Wm. B. Ecrdmans Publishing Company, 1946), p. 107.

6. Jerry L. Glisson, *The Church in a Storm* chapter 9.

7. Plural in the Greek.

8. Brackets mine.

9. Robert Hamblin, *Triumphant Strangers* (Nashville: Broadman Press, 1982), p. 114.

10. W. T. Conner, *The Epistles of John* (New York: Fleming H. Revell Company, 1928), p. 85.

Chapter Twelve

1. Morris Ashcraft, *The Will of God* (Nashville: Broadman Press, 1980), pp. 122-124.

2. Ibid., pp. 126-127.

3. W. T. Conner, *The Gospel of Redemption* (Nashville: Broadman Press, 1945), p. 56.

4. Ibid., pp. 227-228.

5. Ibid., p. 57.

6. T. B. Maston, *God's Will and Your Life* (Nashville, Broadman Press, 1964), p. 90.

7. Morris Ashcraft, *The Will of God*, p. 101.

8. Brackets mine.